Praise fo

before & after our bo[dies] ... look at time linearly, bu[t] ... together a myriad of places and stories in a cinematic way that constellates to make meaning. The speaker of these poems is attentive to life's most granular moments and paints a visually striking wonderland made from the fabric of these memories. As he writes, "i direct the air within the air / i light the colors inside their reflections." These poems pay homage to New Orleans, to lovers, to spirit, to family, and to the body in all its sweet and stormy iterations. *before & after our bodies* is a collection you will find yourself enraptured in every time you pick it up—a collection you will return to in which you will always, delightfully, uncover new, dazzling, heart-filled gems every time you read it.

–Isabella DeSendi, *Through the New Body & Someone Else's Hunger*

Plastic in an orca's stomach! Catfish and fingers! Flashes of orange! How one falls upwards, the sky-as-time-curtain rolling past us! Being inside these poems is a bit like being in the middle of a beautiful, sensory-rich painting where the forms are emergent and ever-changing. What I love about these poems is how energetic they read, even if what is being said is hard, there is an underlying current of joyfulness and liveliness and gratitude. The poet writes: "i had to lose everything to learn that nothing is ever lost," and the poet's generous reach for family, history, time, and home is rewarded again and again. The reader is spun, but never disoriented, and held in the lines as if they were anchors.

– Megan Fernandes, *I Do Everything I'm Told*

Introspective and incantatory, SaintDenisSanchez's debut collection is an evocative critique of what it means to be a subject of an empire in decay, what it means to be a soul in an agnostic world, and what it means to mean among the meaningless. This is a book of transformation that should be on every poetry shelf this year and for all time.

–Darrel Alejandro Holnes, *Stepmotherland*

Phil SaintDenisSanchez has composed not only a sustained, unabashed love letter to New Orleans but also a contemporary Whitmanesque catalog of larger American experience. Here, the speaker's home city becomes a jumping point to interrogate this country's ever-present colonial legacy: "even if the Gulf rises and swallows the whole city to the hilt / these streets can't be unnamed." And yet these interrogations—summoned through a collage of familial and historical figures—maintain intimacy through "the clouds & my lips & / the catfish & my fingers & / my grandmother & her stories." Though SaintDenisSanchez's ambition towards (or perhaps: beyond) a self-portrait of the body is structured as a cascading song cycle, these poems still read us into moments of quiet—especially in the elegy written for the poet's brother, which whispers, "the way you flew from that roof / & / split your skull on the street / like falling in love." This is a work that demonstrates eros as both lurid and sincere, with a speaker who is not just content to witness the sublime but must embrace it directly through the music of language itself.

–Tawanda Mulalu, *Please Make Me Pretty, I Don't Want to Die*

An homage to New Orleans and an ode to ancestral histories and the legacies we carry, *before & after our bodies* paints an exquisite portrait of grief and rapture, destruction and celebration, heartbreak and love, existing simultaneously against the backdrop of empire, hurricanes, and New York City landscapes. With equal parts swagger and vulnerability, SaintDenisSanchez claims the body's paradoxes, its weight and its magnificence. "i had to lose everything to learn that nothing is ever lost," he writes, and "i'd been heartbroken my whole life / but so has everyone i've ever met." Through lyrical voyages across time, SaintDenisSanchez intimates the ways that history and the future are always with us in the present moment. Fate is a mythical time warp that mixes the inevitable with the enigmatic. His clairvoyant verse contemplates the violence that patriarchy enacts on men before they ever laid hands on another. "i wasn't even a teenager when that cop slammed / my high head on the hood of his car ... i wasn't even a teenager when i was told *men are trash* so what was i to become." Through vivid self-portraits with a voice that insists on renewed possibility, this is an inventive debut that dreams beyond the forces of hegemony toward love and liberation, that reclaims the body in all its astonishing glory.

–Cat Wei, "Best of the Net" nominated poet and writer

before & after
our bodies

before & after our bodies

poems by

Phil SaintDenisSanchez

Button Publishing Inc.
Minneapolis
2025

BEFORE & AFTER OUR BODIES
POETRY
AUTHOR: Phil SaintDenisSanchez
COVER DESIGN: Coral Black
COVER PHOTO: Pete Longworth

◇

ALL RIGHTS RESERVED

© 2025 by Phil SaintDenisSanchez

◇

Published by Button Poetry
Minneapolis, MN 55418 | http://www.buttonpoetry.com

Manufactured in the United States of America
PRINT ISBN: 978-1-63834-203-8
EBOOK ISBN: 978-1-63834-112-3
AUDIOBOOK ISBN: 978-1-63834-111-6

First printing

*Because what you heard, or will hear, is true: I wrote /
a better hour onto the page / & watched the fire take it back.*

Ocean Vuong

Table of Contents

self-portrait before & after my body   5

**impossibly young & waiting for a body:
New Orleans & away from New Orleans**

monarchs are the communication medium for when i die   9

self-portrait waiting for a body (nine & a half Royal)   12

New Orleans at four   15

lucid second line   17

everything royal for a moment   22

preface to Camille 1969 & still   26

Camille 1969 & still   27

[the American dream is a ch-ch-ch-ch-chopper]   29

watch out for falling bullets   30

story of my brother's ghost   33

losing my body & other initiations

middle school & other initiations   37

duplex for escaping my body when my body can't escape ...   43

middle school & other initiations redux rant   44

empires always fall

time wings i: this name my grandmother gave me   49

time wings ii: empires always fall   53

the ecstasy of betrayal & other etymologies   57

New York & beyond New York

[we made love on a Brooklyn rooftop under the midsummer sun while Papi watched]   65

Phil, my love   67

but if fire   68

La Pucelle (Planned Parenthood)   70

New York: the portal to paradise at the end of time   71

oceans:
ecosystem & apex

Thai snake bite   77

Cecil's long shadow   81

who are you to question the exigency of a bicycle?   85

i'm back on Cape Cod, eating lobster rolls again   87

you know   88

we publish come hell & high water   89

remembered to forget that i'm god just like you

infinite duplex with eight gates & a coda:
as you requested, *a written recap of our night*   97

self-portrait as past lives   101

recovering my body

spell to name the spell   107

self-portrait recovering my body:
spell to bring the body back   108

poems as spells

naming cats   113

letter to my godson Kaimel on his third birthday   115

City of Gods (i – xi)   125

the spirits who feast with us

duplex with four gates for Rex:
prayers to a new cat god passing in my arms on Easter Sunday   143

Juchereau Oxóssi Saint Denis / Maria Oxúm Sánchez   146

i got back from Bahia (all the saudades)   148

how are the laddies?   150

land back on Tchoupitoulas (no one else can bring my music)   151

for my brother prelude & epilogue

for my brother   157

Notes   161

Acknowledgments   177

About the Author   179

Book Recommendations from the Author   181

before & after
our bodies

self-potrait before & after my body

        watched

    from both sides

my body is

    the film

        capturing

    the flight of

time against it

impossibly young & waiting for a body:
New Orleans & away from New Orleans

They were awake ... while most of America slept. And those awake are the nightmares of the sleepers.

Rachel Kushner

monarchs are the communication medium for when i die

for my grandmother Mere

Never has there been a more respectable hurricane, provided with all the portents, predictions, omens, etc. The awful sunrise—no one could fail to take a warning from it—the hovering black spirit bird, the man of war, just one, comme il faut.

New Orleanian Painter Walter Anderson on Hurricane Betsy, which he rode out tied to a tree on the highest dune on Horn Island

i.

the clouds & my lips &
    the catfish & my fingers &
        my grandmother & her stories:
all Mississippi-burnt marshmallows
    by the pool & lounging
        along the Gulf coast & manning it,
my grandmother's gaze keeping waterspouts
    from touching down too close to me
        allowing me the space to enjoy my catch in peace
a tiny sun in my belly quieted by sweet tea & new tales
      go print your new piece & read it to me, my lamby
i steer hurricanes from interrupting us
    by knowing just how to ride the eye
i just found out my heart stopped while my mom was
giving birth to me & i see now how that feeling never left me
    it lifts me above the heavy clouds
        in moments
            when the barometric pressure drops too low
    it begins to begin
    a flash of orange & black from Mexico
    the first wings of October
    falling upward opposite the
    leaves up north sharing their shade

        do people also need to die to keep the air around us fertile?
        here they are gathering flame & giving way to a flock
        Mere's been waiting for that flicker
        of how the dead perceive the living & i embed it in my body as a
prayer for my unraveling & the becoming that might follow

you know butterflies are the communication medium for when i die
    watch for butterflies
        especially monarchs

      we speak through them,
      curve into their coastal margins
      parading through the air just above the swells
      like Creole royalty holding our ground as it
      recedes beneath us—
      least of all a throne—
      leaving us with nothing to grip,
      but the heart-quickening needed for what's coming

ii.

we've been windbeaten to ready
for the years of this coming century will be divided by its storms
beneath Mere's print of Jonah bursting from the whale
i lie in bed
        throbbing a beat inside the terror of what i've called to me
in moments i let the mad waves' break breach the berm
        wetlands absorbing a new night's surge
to say that men need to destroy & rebuild
        is to say Laska likes chasing tennis balls up grassy hills,
            or like saying i finish to our videos

i can barely maintain the boundaries of my body
        on beaches, in bars, in The Woods she presses up against me
            & touches what she wants
another noun becomes a verb & she lingers on it
        i wait under the weight of language bodies

        piling up in this battle
    the costumes of The Leopard Society calling my skin
promising to save me from the monstrous hunger if
      i don't mind eating my own
         it's not in me
    but in me still
my antennae with all they can feel still hidden
      in my dream panoply
          i tell Mere everything i hope to do with my life
      & get a quick scolding to wake me
well, you better get started
      & i see how close i am to emerging from the sea
         or swallowing it
    time a trade wind in my migration
      or a lighthouse before the crash

we're all one sail to Horn Island from being Walter Anderson during Betsy:
    a body & a waist with a skiff tethered to it
    two lungs & a chest roped to a black mangrove tree
    even on the highest dune
    the ocean wet all the way to both nipples spilling
      wind-whipped seed & milk frothed to every wavelength at once
interlocking watercolors unveiled where the pelican first appeared white[1]

---

[1]   After Walter Anderson's *Pelican and Waves (Horizontal Pelican)*

self-portrait waiting for a body
(nine & a half Royal[2])

i keep trying to tell you what happened that night
i was there waiting for a body
beside me the same spirits who
crushed the river crescent to a city
they curved the land to their liking
reflected their likeness in a new country
far from Yorubaland
if you've ever received them
you know the weight of their light
the drag & the sway they demand
my mother said she knew that night
      she also said she knew within
           ten minutes that she would marry my father

was there as well
      in his mind & less certain again
but everyone knew
whatever body i was given
      this one is more cub than babe
i took my first words from animals
i painted my kindergarten self-portrait in my black jaguar costume

Antoinette beside me at Mardi Gras as Raggedy Ann
      even at four
it was always so obvious she would marry a balding Episcopalian
        complain about his receding hairline to dinner guests
           & birth kids who sing opera

the incessant songs of Congo Square
seeped into nine & a half Royal

---

[2] Another name for 912 Royal St in the French Quarter where my parents were living when my mom got pregnant with me.

        choirs of children
            asking *what is royalty?*
with crushed coke cans taped to the bottom of their Reeboks
        trapping beats for Popeyes,
tennies barely holding in the tongue
      but still snapping stars into the *kat er* sky
         before the clouds roll in & release
poured over & deep purple / nine & a half Royal held strong
i was there waiting for a body
      but i was not alone
warriors from the Caddo nation heeded
      my seventh-great-grandfather's beads once more
         to lead them to refuge again
         to sweet water again
            after the Red River flooded their fields
            he led the Natchitoches tribe
            to new homes north of Lake Pontchartrain
                where they feasted on crawfish étouffée
                    & Beaujolais
                until they returned to
                    their ancestral lands
                    they tattooed thick snakes round
                    his legs & named him
                        Kadolahoapi:
                          Chief Big Leg
                  widens the
                  family tree beneath me
            before my next becoming

my new body a battleground promised
to my beloved's mouth,
her words clear as quick creeks:
you taste like victory
even digested in her stomach
      like the residue of someone from a dream
          waking with a distant ache
              out of reach of storms & horizons

place me curving in the way sea meets land for miles
from here i can see a form coasting towards me,
my body & the questions it brings:

who am i before & after it?

will my sex defy me?

what is my blood?
& why did my seventh-great Manuela free Big Leg
        from her step-grandfather's prison?
                they fled Mexico for Louisiana
                      & started a new line

what is royalty?
is it what we can't touch?
or is it Lead Belly singing of the Titanic?
everywhere in Louisiana
i still hear the harmonies of Angola's chain gangs

if you thirst for proof that the past never ceases
        put your lips on my new body
                & drink

New Orleans at four

my father broke a glass milk jug fresh over the skull
    of an armed robber
        in our driveway
            on a trip back from Langenstein's,
    knocked him out cold
        stomped his head into the concrete
            took his gun & flight
    while my mother read us Creole stories from Mere's books
        in Mimi's attic
Mimi was busy proving time wrong at ninety-four & blew death off
    for another decade before she finally said why not
Mere was in 1822 watching Marie Laveau's daughter
    free slaves from the auction block
    before Laveau was shipped off to Santiago to save her from
        the fear of her power
    Mere wrote their stories in chalk crosses
        & taught her students at Tulane the same dialect
on the steps of my other childhood home Pop called the sonofabitch
    with the chopper in his belly a *sonofabitch*
    threw cash in his face & walked away for he still
        held the real heat
        he made it rain before storm clouds rolled in &
            brought the four o'clock relief
        (summer scorched / made the bricks sweat /
        summer heavy as new sin deep inside you)
    World War II never stops in his head or on his television
        that man can watch the fuck out some D-Day docs

the arch of oak trees over Saint Charles trying in vain
    to teach me patience
Domelise's serving fully-dressed po' boys with glass root beers
brass burning syncopation into the air
infinite ivy fingers reaching up a building-side to sky
brother i'm home again / sister i'm home again

    i dressed as a black jaguar for Mardi Gras
        the first costume i chose for myself
            floats showered me in beaded luck
                they saw me
                they felt me
Amy on her long four-block bus ride back to the Magnolia
        blessed, sweet-scented war zone
Mable on repeat: *that lil four-year-old chile*
        gonna be president one day
impossibly young, i wandered through Audubon Park
        identifying mushrooms:
                chanterelles, wood ears, even amanitas,
                      telling my mother which ones were safe to eat

lucid second line

the smell of brass smoldering in his
sleep
    he woke to the fire of the parade
       grabbed his horn
          & took aim at Shamarr
      out the window of his room
   with one hand
Pop lifted me up by the nape of my neck for walking in front of a lady
painted & open at Zulu
like the lion cub i donned
he placed me back into the pride of the beat
wrapped in never-ending notes
    for death & for spring
       for the fattening before Lent
from the wishes of Pans & princesses bouncing free
'til the brain bursts
inside, tell me what you see:
a lucid second line still possible to ride
it's how you enter

walk into any shop on Magazine
the sweet *what you need, sha*s pour

the sweet *what you need, sha*s
    for the ease of the whole city in one big boat
      gliding in with all the saints

we're in Butler's:
a shack losing its roof in the black pearl
my cousin waving defiant in the middle of the dance floor
oblivious to every shoulder leaning his way
matching Ice Cube, MC Ren, Easy-E, & Dr. Dre
line for line
in perfect flow
Fuck tha Police

searching for yey
from strangers
finally a dread with gold teeth offers
if he'll give him cash first
waiting outside for gilded grills to return
i tell my cousin he's never coming back
he has to, he tells me
he can't stay in that busted shanty all night
people must go back home eventually
it's how the world works
& if he doesn't have the coke
i'll trip him when he tries to run
like his feet are cosmic magnets

we pull all American music & spirits south to the toes of the boot
like water down the drain of a bathtub
we're the center of the spiral
we reverse & hurricane it all through the other cities & towns
the lands dry & calm before us
   be grateful
   without us America would have no music & no spirits
absinthe from the Old Absinthe House in the alley
   the sugar cube aflame in the green
    repeating ghosts beating a blue drum clean of its air
line for line
in perfect polyrhythm
   each syncopation leaning back off the pulse
right where it needs to lie;
we're the first American town to measure time by storms

my uncle's throw from the float still until we choose to blink again
   then the beads rushed our faces & necks
my uncle's throw from the float still until we remember motion
   then the doubloons bouncing off our teeth
    we could still be there
   no eyelids, no gravity

                    my cousin & i
                            ecstasy at high tide
                            perched on the drum colors of the parade

sailing the winds of Carnival season
after Brees threaded a holy sphere through the cover two
        into two praying palms
        to Stills
        to still the wailing
        for one Sunday, all the churches stopped shaking
after twenty-two intercepted our city's lost son & took him home
        then we knew we'd be marching in

but are we gonna get there with our bodies?
        maybe not
                but we need our legs, our feet to second line

we need our mouths, our lips to consume
to wake to freedom from Rose's chicory café au lait
to burn for blackened cocodril from the grill
        cooled by alligator pears stuffed with crab meat

my great-grandfather Pere whispering the reign
of his grandfather Isaac Newton Marks
my third great
King of Carnival
embers threatening the throne
        suspended with song over the streetcar rails
                run parallel, never touch
leading the unification movement:
        tinder merging with wind
                waiting for a spark to carry

my hometown is one fire after another
street taken over & falling apart

      give in to the ghost dance
      give in to the ghost
      dance the ghost
      ghost the dance
      into the ghost dance

Denis formed from Dionysus in the veins of family trees
      blessed by the African gods that spill spirits
      we drink on every corner 'til all we see are goddesses
      my aunt is slurring my name again at Bacchus
          & i know my response will just be spilled
wine on the river barge
      staining the poque chips with my fingers' want
i put my life on the line
      before the turn
          into a new king's death

what does his funeral sound like?
Taj Mahal with ten tubas
textured by flambeaux torches & feathers
circling the face of Chief Becate Batiste
      mirrored everywhere, especially in flight,
          each bird a film

my memories of the
State Palace Theater
      cascading from wedding cake balconies
          rolling in a sea
touching everything & being touched
a woman finally breaking free
i love Black people
& in his kindness
i love white people
but to pretend to care about a decaying baby's bones from another century
      when you have a body filled with work & beats

                lit & lit again by the American sun
                        answering the call for a country & a culture
is an impossible offering;
best to bury it & let its cries drown in the ghost crowds

swelling through the sousaphone
thickened by the bass drum
curling to the trumpet
this could finally be the wave
that carries us away for good
if the world were made anew
it would be in the line
shooting this march to shore
Tremé,
Hot Eight,
Rebirth:
they all promise nightly,
& even though they keep their tone
        riding a crescent night
                where we choose the colors & the meter
                still the sun enters
                        & asks for a rest

maybe this revolution i keep living in my head isn't asleep
but a brain fire we can't quiet
a heat we can't cool
L'Ouverture sparked the sale of Louisiana
        & launched steamboats carrying our name to Natchez
even as we spread
with the river it rages
& washes away our faces
krewes still float expressions
every mask a triumph
        in a dream we stalk loudly

everything royal for a moment

every fourth
on the beach
my grandfather's bonfire
    melting marshmallows
        melting chocolate
           over our hands
raising lanterns up over the Gulf
dragging our feet to scare the skates
    while fishing for flounder
        lanterns up
my grandfather gathers us for ghost stories:
in the sixties
on the same sands where we now stand
walked pale creatures who thought they were real & white at once
they banded together to try to chase the Yoruba spirits from their
nests in the dunes, as if they could be swayed,
raising sand high as it could go
royal terns
swooping
raising sand high as it would go

the columns of my childhood home
rise in the twelfth ward over the twelfth night
    that never gifts another morning
        caught mid-breath waiting for the final present

i walked along the water to air my heart in the wind
    in hopes the lovesick would blow away
        saw my eight-year-old self sailing the Gulf solo
            a gust swung the boom into
                my skull & split my forehead on the centerboard
i spun round the singular drop of the ocean shelf
    watching my blood begin to dominate
        the ocean spray at the bottom of my sunfish

    thinking there's no greater gift than being able to free your
bones of your thoughts & let them all pour out into the earth & steep
    no that's not what i thought then
    i thought
       how do i get back to shore?
       how do i get back to shore
         with this much blood in my boat?
i thought of freeing bones that night in bed as my father read me
a story about Zeus breaking open his brain to birth his daughter:
wisdom

Sophie spilled her head on the glass coffee table
    at Louis Armstrong Airport
      on our way to France
three cannon bursts from Bastille Day

we left her behind & went anyway
we left the fireworks representing gunfire & the gunfire imitating
    celebration behind

for a castle in the land of La Pucelle d'Orléans with
a moat & a courtyard
    that threatened to never give way to a dining hall
      no matter how many steps i took
my mind burned from me
by VVS Hennessy from
    19th-century wooden barrels
     & Belgian women with breasts out
      impossibly in the noon sun
       refusing to admit their miracle

while my brother was being buried with a letter i wrote for him:
   a piece of my heart is being sawed off & buried with you

i left him behind & went anyway

i returned to a country still playing war
while my city lived it

let me tell you a few things about New Orleans:
no one really says *N'awlins*

& you can only say New Orleans with a lean in song
do you know what it means?
do you know what it means to need to mix codeine,
       Sprite, & a watermelon Jolly Rancher into purple lean
             in a Styrofoam cup?
      so everything can be royal for just a moment?
      so maybe a moment of cool?
              but that demand is a demon no medicine can clean
hot boys on so much lean they need their stomach pumped

my people
      living in a shotgun
            waiting to be pumped back out into the river
                  gutted the lower ninth ward

mothers asking every day what happened to that boy?
we all know but we don't talk
      not in my city
           we don't talk about that
even as it's destined from the red stripes & the blue fold
most American cities birthed crips & bloods
      when they came from the West & conquered lands

we got bloods & crips
      when they expanded east
           & ghosts stole their flags
                their names
                      the breath beneath their chants
            & replanted them in new faces
            new buildings
              new lungs

Piru painted on a five point star
curves to a cast iron fleur-de-lis
        mounting the cemetery's gate
        mounting the cemetery's gait
green crosses tatted between my brothers' eyebrows
        proclaiming five sixty-day murders circling for an eternity

& since Xangô rules this town while disguised as
Saint John the Baptist
        oxygen overcomes our blood
                runs through arteries
        never veins

saturated with o
o
        o
                oh
lord
        why
                oh
lord
        why
                us
lord
        oh
                lord

the awe that never dies
& you ask to be pumped full of it
so you stay crimson
        even stretched
                with the thick of night
        even waking alone to a new independence &
                the embers of a dying fire

preface to Camille 1969 & still

after Christopher Dunlap's painting *Haymaker 002*

in paint strokes
the sunrise over the Nile River banks
    mirrored at the surface
        & flipped vertically at its line of reflection
    so the sun burns in against itself from the edges
        towards an open skycenter where the winds build

in pain strokes
the hollow beneath my ribcage
    painted on a canvas
        hung on my brother's wall

the hollow beneath my ribcage
    an eye waiting in the darkness
waiting to flood far past what we need to irrigate the river valley

i'm okay & i'm not okay at all

sure i can wear faces with the best
    but there's a crisis gathering heavy in my chest
        when the wind whips through my heart
    i have no skin / no ribcage
chambers singing bright as sun on flowers reflecting back
    the color that is not there

i'm still hawking wind
    in search of space
with my cousin riding Pop's boat 'cross Bay Saint Louis
    docking in its harbor
        for raw oysters & Red Stripes at the Blind Tiger
we're kings in this land
    & you'd have to be raving mad to question that
unfortunately nearly everyone's raving mad in these storms

        most of all i'm in the eye
        so am i the calm or the cause?

Camille 1969 & still

i don't really know why i'm sad
        but part of it is the way everyone pretends they can't
            feel the storm gathering
you don't need to have been shot in the knee
        in the Battle of New Orleans,
           rocking on Marie Laveau's roof in a rocking chair,
        for your bones to quake before
            what is before us

i found M reading at the DMV & saw that
she's sad in the same ways i'm sad
so it was easy for us to wash away our sadness together
        like seashells repeating the ocean
when i left her it amplified our sadness
        but she is you until this hurricane ends

& the past never ceases to exist if you reach out far enough towards it
        it's kept kinetic by your touch
the ghost is the truth
        in times like these
in times like these
        the Chauvins still cling to the highest branch
            of my grandparents' oak
        Johnny to the capsized boat flung all the way down to the
            railroad tracks
            Diedra is still drowning having just learned to crawl
                the dog's barks stilled & swallowed
                    Camille always raging
                        always August 17th, 1969
                    always still again

Mere & Pop talk of Camille like her winds just left
but couldn't possibly return

    the pier was destroyed for at least the twelfth time
    the pier long again into the ocean
      about to be destroyed again, always

Mere & Pop talk of Camille like she's the same storm as all the others
    they also pretend Flanders III is the same dog as Flanders I &
    Flanders II
      all little black Schipperkes gifting new
        nothings to bitch about
         your grandmother up there raising sand about
         the dog finna get
         out so i shut the door
         i shut the door on you to keep out the floods
           but doors don't block water
              they only delay it

Mere & Pop talk of Camille like her winds were unlike any others
    but Bob's boat sat in the boat shed waiting to
    sail round the world
      but it didn't touch salt water
         'til Katrina came & carried it out of sight

Mere & Pop talk of Camille like her winds just left
but couldn't possibly return
    even ripped apart & scattered
      our family rises again as a modern-day Osiris
    always sewn together in the end

but Camille's in my chest
& i think of kneeling before you again

[the American dream is a ch-ch-ch-ch-chopper³]

the American dream is a ch-ch-ch-ch-chopper
    with tattooed arms on the handles,
        behind them
            breasts & hair clean against the wind

the American dream is a ch-ch-ch-ch-chopper
    ripping through bodies
        like the drum in *Machine Gun*
bands of gypsies invading from god knows what star

the American dream is a ch-ch-ch-ch-chopper
    & they don't call my hometown chopper city
    for the fucking police helicopters circling nightly,
    voodoo chile
    we do sixty-day murders & let rex Xangô
    sort the ghosts out in the overflowing parade
        rioting in the cemeteries,
        in my grandmother's house,
        on my ancestors' streets,
        on Xangô's streets
            horse hooves beat a second line beat
    on cobblestone
        the sparks they create turn
    everything fulgurant
        like bullets again & again

---

3   *cuz my seconds, minutes, hours go to the almighty dollar /*
     and the almighty power of that ch-ch-ch-ch-chopper

    Mr. Carter

watch out for falling bullets

Watch out for falling bullets.

*My aunt calling out to my cousins & me
as we left the house one New Year's Eve.*

    burners to the stars torching seconds from the old year
        as if nothing ever falls
            &
    gravity is just a joke passing through our ribcage
to a quickening beat
    in celebration
the lovesick return from the sky
every new year a newborn
    bless the drum roll's brain again
never can tell
    when the windfall
        never can see
so watch the heavens
every television & radio warns
every third commercial before the first of the year:
falling bullets kill
the gunfire on the eve is as inevitable as fireworks
we were as fire streaking between the car & my cousin's house
so as not to get caught

beloved, you rained down through me
when i asked you not to
left me no choice but to return

i'm back in my Mimi's city,
my Mere's city,
my last love's favorite place to swing,
my tongue finally lazy & alive
trying to taste what's wet again

the will of the Magnolia trees through the air
    when the windfall burns again
leaves the taste of gunpowder in the gumbo filé
    thickening Mable's roux
remember whodi?
Rest In Power
remember, whodi:
    the clip's lighter than banana peels when it's done again
you told me you love to feel its weight on your face
i love to press it against your cheek
    when you offer it
        until my burden becomes your ache
            i transmute ammunition in this way
love, the next hit
    the next hit might be the one
        i never return from
i seek it & i fear it: the heat

every new year, black-eyed peas, collard greens, &
    hunting for bullets on my cousin's roof
ghost stories for the hunted & despair again
    again the rain into the stairwell
        we finally found the culprit:
            steel its trajectory
                from the leak to the floor
when the lovefall comes once more
    it's not the winds but the waters
        that will demand reparations
& you better be prepared to pay
    & you better be prepared to
        dance from your wheelchair
on the porch of your shotgun
    stripped of your color
        bright purple & gold
            umbrellas lapping at each instrument
                tongues through the clouds
exhaling your dying breath

        before your next,
drowning before the sun slowly dries
        the porch of your shotgun
where no one is safe
        & if they are safe,
                they aren't where you want to be

& maybe on the eve of a new year
when the windfall comes again
kann lanmoutombé la encore
when the lovefall comes again
kann lanmoutombé la encore
when the lovefall comes again
it may not be a storm
        but a glance towards the clouds clearing
bearing a brightening & a darkening
& it will demand music,
it will demand music
        & you better be prepared to sing
tunes over the balcony
        wrought iron over the quarter
1999 'til i die
1999 'til i die
every year as it turns again
pretending to be new
        each eye opening & asking for a waterfall
        each blink cascading the time-drip
i had to stop
        & ask you to stop being so stunning
so i could return to music again

in the center of the note
        where the sound waves
                most like a circle
        for a space
safe from falling bullets

story of my brother's ghost

My brother Carrick died when I was ten. I remember the moment I found out so vividly: my family had just gotten back from the beach, the house phone (R.I.P.) was ringing on repeat, my mom answered & let out an animalistic scream unlike anything I'd ever heard. The noise my mostly soft-spoken but quietly fierce, subtly owllike, trauma therapist mother let loose feels like it's still echoing in my chest sometimes. So that you can picture my brother: he was 6'2" (6'4" in my mind), exquisitely angel-faced, brilliant in many ways— his AI coding at MIT just one example, hugely generous, effortlessly magnetic & charming, athletic, & an avid explorer, consumer, & lover of music. You probably think I'm getting carried away eulogizing or idolizing, but I promise you I'm not even really doing him justice; everything I've just said about him was said a thousand times over while he was still alive.

I'd known people who had died before their time, but no one both young & close to me had ever crossed over. It was my first time feeling the full force of a sudden, unexpected death's blow. In some ways, he was the closest person in the world to me when he died.

Technically he was my uncle, my mother's youngest brother, but he lived with us in the upstairs of my great-grandmother's house in New Orleans, so we grew up like brothers & calling him anything else wouldn't be right. From a very early age, he put me onto much of the music that shaped me: early Afrobeat like Fela Kuti, hardcore like Bad Brains, dub & ska like Lee *Scratch* Perry, & most of all roots reggae—Burning Spear, Black Uhuru, Jacob Miller & Inner Circle, Peter Tosh, & especially Bob Marley—the acoustic versions of hits, the deep cuts, the rare bootlegs of live concerts.

He fell from a rooftop in the East Village while tripping on acid.

It started about a month after he passed, as I lay down in bed to go to sleep at night, I would start thinking he was asking to come see me. The ask wasn't auditory—it presented just like any other recurring thought. I couldn't tell whether it was real or just my imagination, but it scared me, so I'd always reply in my head, *No, I'm not ready yet.*

The thought was persistent for about a year & a half, every night as I lay in bed it would present itself & I'd always answer the same way, *I'm not ready yet.* Then it started visiting me less & less frequently until the conversations stopped entirely.

Years later, I was nineteen & staying at my maternal grandfather's house for the holidays. A framed picture of Carrick rested on the nightstand beside my bed. As I'm trying to fall asleep, I had the thought again: he's asking to come see me. I had already decided that the thought was just my imagination, a coping mechanism, so what's the harm in saying *yes* this one time?

I lay there waiting to see if my new answer would change anything this time. After five minutes with no response, I told myself I'd proven once & for all that it was just internal dialogue.

Almost immediately after concluding it wasn't real, I felt a powerful energy enter my body, a lightning that held me. It lifted me out of my body so that I hovered three or four feet above my physical form. I was bursting light, a light that subsumed the need to breathe. It felt like an eternity, but it probably only lasted thirty to sixty seconds in "real time." Then the light left me &, rocking back & forth like a feather falling, I eased back into my body.

losing my body & other initiations

The first act of violence that patriarchy demands of males is not violence toward women. Instead patriarchy demands of all males that they engage in acts of psychic self-mutilation, that they kill off the emotional parts of themselves. If an individual is not successful in emotionally crippling himself, he can count on patriarchal men to enact rituals of power that will assault his self-esteem.

bell hooks

middle school & other initiations

i.

the first time i really saw the stars
they hit me / first time they hit me
i really saw the stars
   Pleiades & their oceanic mother
      washed over my nymph body
         still childing idyllic &
            on the cusp of shifting
               constellations

the second strike
   loosened Orion's belt & i saw
     my world fall out of myself

i lay naked on the concrete
   through the rest of the strikes
     while all the stars watched
       & told me i wasn't enough
         in every way
            i wasn't enough

what the fuck is that
   who the fuck is that
     said the stars
       like they were destiny
         but they had human bodies
       & human names like Max
   & Nick
   & Chris

even as they violated me
   from above
     i tried to talk to the gods

     who were also above me
      so who & where was i?
       & how could a child
     know the difference
     between them & the godly sky?

ii.

the words where my lips have been
   the voice my throat would one day make sonorous
     the names my body knew as mine
      there's nothing left of me
       but the afterflash of butterfly wings
      leaving the path

leaving the path is the only way
   to become what i need to become
     i got kicked out of public schools in seventh grade

i'd already been pumping since late that winter anyway
   how did they let me stay after we Bravehearted
    the private school next door
      i told them not to run their mouths
      just cuz they had numbers for
       a brief moment
        the next day
      when their school let out
     we charged them a hundred deep
     & sent everyone fleeing back inside &
  bolting the door
they kept it pushing after that

my best friend hated me
   but we were both wild & uncontrollable
     i heard his dad had connects in Colombia
      & i had friends in places he couldn't walk
       he had five enemies for every friend

                    i was the opposite
                so we were useful to each other
            when he was killed in the middle of a house party
                    for smacking one of his runners around
                        everyone saw it coming
            i heard it was the largest obstruction of justice filing
                    outside of a RICO in the history of the country
                they made the whole house party bury the body
                        & swore them to secrecy

she swore me to secrecy so i can't tell you how much older she was
            when she went down on me in the woods in the summer
                    between eighth & ninth grade
                        but i will tell you she drove us there
she tried to swallow me but i just
            hit throat &   hit the back of throat &   touched throat &
                    some eternal hunger
                        she swallowed the life at the end of desire
                            & told me to watch porn & compare
                                like maybe i have a future,
                                    new eyes,
                                a body worthy of life,
                            & the L i light to lean harder into breath

the L leans me back into the hardest relax
        i drip the coconut oil down the length to slow the light
            let the shine beckon angels
                bathing in the screen
                    i study the bounce
                    freeze the bodies
                            & hold myself up to compare:
                                my width is clear
                                    &
                                i feel my new power
                                    stretch the air
                            hard to say on length
                                i'm almost there

                              but most of
                    all i'm finding beauty where i
                was first taught shame / smooth
            with the turquoise & amethyst veins
          light beneath my olive skin
       my purple radiating deep night is quiet
& needing nothing

i relax into god's mind
lord i lean into the sun
          even when it's not out
                    you can be who you want to be i tell myself
                         you don't have to be powerless
                         & i soak in my power
                         still i awake depowered & shaking it
                    wondering where it went
               its states seem infinite & i oscillate with them
i count at least eight

at least eight arrests that i can remember
          the first was for grand theft auto
                    but i was twelve & just a backseat passenger
                         they thought i'd break when i came home to
                         a detective at my family's kitchen table
                              the next year
                                   but i was just moving ounces
                                        &
                                   i knew they didn't have
                         anything on me
                              they just wanted me
                         for whom i knew & my infinite time

god i felt like i knew everyone
          Freddy & i laughed ourselves through the smoke
               the last time he sold me a qp
                    he gave me an extra bag for free
                    right before Samuel Sheinbein

                      & Needle
                              killed him with a sawed-off
                 & burned the body
Sheinbein fled to Israel & the U.S. somehow lost
          the extradition battle to a country whose existence it funds
              i heard about my dead friend on the news
                  for a full year
                        including from my dad
                                when he was in Gaza
                      while bombs in the background
            decorated his voice on the phone
                as it carried across
                      so many walls
                            to get to me
          their thunder signaling so many deaths
                  Ahmed wasn't even a teenager

iii.

i wasn't even a teenager when i was
hotboxing the playhouse in
        my grandmother's backyard
                let the front door yawn smoke
                      & hopped the fence
on my way to Martin's for Muffaletta
i heard fireworks that weren't fireworks
i saw fire dance from one car window to another
        like when you love someone so much
                you turn their world to nothing
                      but light
                light leaving a seashell repeating the ocean
                    the ocean how i wept

how i wept when Carlos didn't make it
        he was my favorite Carlos, too
                big Carlos tried to show me his dick
                while we were high in Brian's backyard

                              i got a glimpse & told him he wasn't doing
                                    himself any favors
                              but the Carlos who got shot in front of his grandmother's
                        building in the summer between seventh & eighth grade
                              had such a good heart
                                    & was way more fun to get high with
                                          he was in love with V
                                                just like everyone else
                                                      but he still gave me
                                                props after i hooked up with her
                                          behind the tennis wall
                                    during Social Studies
                              she gave me slow blessings & slow love
                  let love slow / Carlos with the good heart
got aired out in front of his abuela's building
                  left him full of quiet windows
                              & good questions
                                    good questions leaking all over the
                              street / himself / every /
            where / beyond
himself
                  where the brightest star is left alone

in a clear mirror i gaze up &
down the length of my lost self,
wonder where i've been hiding inside myself

let unseen beauty clear my path,
            keep me safe in this dark world
                        taste the victory spilling from me slowly, love
slow love, i've beautiful'd my way back to you
            for good
                        this time

duplex for escaping my body when my body can't escape ...

after Jericho Brown

one day i'll be heard i hear myself think
as i project myself out of my body

        sometimes i leave my body while still alive
        does this change the way time unfolds across it?

does this change how their hands unfurl across it?
i'm not dreaming them forcing my nakedness

        still a child, but i'm dreaming towards death
        death is just a time machine we all use

listen, death is just a time machine we all use
i remember a never-violated future

        i remember a future where my voice reigns
        for now just *hold where you are like a baby*

hold where you are like a baby, i
tell myself one day i will be heard

middle school & other initiations redux rant

i wasn't even a teenager when i realized this empire we live in will never last
i wasn't even a teenager when i started walking out of Social Studies class
    i couldn't hear those half-truths anymore
i wasn't even a teenager when that cop slammed
    my high head on the hood of his car
i wasn't even a teenager when the stars stripped me naked
    & mocked me
i wasn't even a teenager when i was told *men are trash*
    so what was i to become
        a kind of man that doesn't quite exist yet
i wasn't even a teenager when the only man i could've
    emulated fell from a roof & left this plane
i wasn't even a teenager when i stopped trusting men
    Mark passed me the joint i thought was just weed
        but it was laced with boat / he told me afterwards
            we're going to the moooooonnnn
            in the woods i watched
            the trees wave while he laughed
so when my friend roofied me at
    my own house party & left me naked
        with her lipstick all over me
so when another friend lied on my tongue while
    i tried to comfort her
so when the theater dancer got mad at me
    because her girlfriend was
        flirting with me / she made sure
            my sex paid for it
so when the Special Victims Unit detective told me she couldn't
    go after her despite her crime
        because they have to come up with the positive
            identification on their own

        i awoke to a world where i had no one left to trust

i awoke to a world where i saw how you were only hunted
if you were secretly powerful

i awoke to see how everyone unsure of their own power
would try endlessly to blind you to yours

i awoke to a world where i saw how my one deep touch
could change someone forever

empires always fall

Je est un autre.

Arthur Rimbaud

time wings i:
this name my grandmother gave me

sometimes i fly through time free of body, worries, & ancestral lines,
but for the other times my grandmother gave me this name
carved from the roots of our family tree

light like magnolia trees burning sunwardly
the whole sky above me on perfect timing
clouds, rain, & church bells making musical hyperbole

Saint like a proven miracle
Denis comes from Dionysus dripping sin
Sanchez zipped back up in holy light

she dropped my name upon me halo'd
in her mouth, palindrome'd in its meaning,
light between the letters, a quiet sieve

i taste only the honey-notes they let in / you made it through
the sounds of ancestors & angels guarding my future
so i know my grandmother loves you / from the sky / i slow blink you

into my vision & see your full lips start
hungering / hear you say my full name /
full with the love that *touches & changes*

everything / you should know everything
my grandmother gives me is apotropaic
America can be a death cult, beloved, & this name is

protecting me from it / can we start
a new nation? *nation* born from *natus*
the Latin past *nasci* means *to be born*

every nation is a slow forever birthing until its fall
we need to go back to the seed to finally touch
light / i told the Hoodoo priest, Chiron, i want to

heal my ancestral lines / *that's a noble idea*
he told me, *but it doesn't really work like that*
everyone's ancestors have wounds & sins

the healing works best flowing downstream so learn to
receive more / to heal yourself is to invite them into that healing
you have six offerings to make before you leave New Orleans:

/ write a letter filled with poetry to your father &
read it to the mighty Mississippi then cast it in the river
this is your offering to Odin

/ bibliomancy in Saint Louis Cathedral for the questions in your heart / leave
tobacco at Congo Square in exchange for its dirt on your ancestral altar
/ offer twelve crab cakes & rum sprayed from your lips to Xangô who claims

the whole city as his child / for Santa Muerte & your Mexican egun
leave a terracotta bowl filled with spring water, seven coins, three
sunflowers, & three white roses by the Archangel Michael sculpture

near the entrance of Saint Roch Cemetery No. 2
at 1725 Music / that you may always be
in right relationship with death

/ place three pennies on the corner of Saint Philip &
Royal on the block you were conceived for Papa
Legba & ask him to help you see with the eyes of

your heart / you have a voice like thunder, with weight,
a prophetic voice that does things / but what does that
mean & what should i do with it? *prepare for love like*

*you've never prepared for anything, or you'll be prepared for
love* / as i lay the third penny between the tiles bearing
the *A* & the *L* on the sidewalk of Royal St

my tasks completed right before my departing
flight / the sky opens like a heart past its limit:
suddenly & fully, rain thick like a limb built to

stretch what's possible / in this downpour, thunder
drums all around the car on the way to Louis
Armstrong airport / once at my gate i devour a

fried green tomato, shrimp remoulade po' boy
& feel wide open / it's finally all starting to break open
to what i knew it could be & anything could happen

we're fucking on your balcony as the sun sets sienna &
gilded across the Empire State watching planes coast upward
i see the summer coming in the distance like a new

generation ready to burst from me / one day our children will
laugh at emojis & dismiss our emoji art only to have later
generations revive & celebrate it / they'll awe at iMessages in

museums / we use telepathy now in this wing of the future &
all the ones stretched out beyond it / your eyes bend out the cool
sky & pull everything into their vision / when we come

together like time could take flight from our mind forever
or like time could briefly embody the sky / the pink
passing gradation at the skyline cools the burnt sienna to

a pale yellow past the plane wing &
maybe time is gliding alongside it
this poem started inside you as

we watched planes fly by / so of course i pick it back up
on the flight to Miami with your head on my shoulder /
my grandmother would've loved you / just like

she hated the way so many desperately
pretend to understand people
who travel outside of their perceptions

in my sky-drip, my name flows down heaven first
ancestors pouring from ancestors flowing from
ancestors woven into the air before me

i funnel myself through their air tunnel untouched
& touching everything like empire
touches & changes everything

but unlike empire their wind opens hearts & bodies
/ on Miami Beach the pale faces in front of us are
Lakeview'ing so hard: *in grade school this one kid kept*

trying to tell us everything about monarch butterflies
& i was like i don't give a fuck about monarch butterflies
& this is how they stay stuck in the chrysalis

Mere would've laughed at them so hard / the body that i'm being
here now is the body that is asking for you open, melting from
a pleasure glacier, & no longer concerned with the naming of things

time wings ii:
empires always fall

does time still exist?
                        no, we slept it all away

you reply to me from my bed / before
dawn / i rise from dreams ravenous

order espresso with my Caesar salad
from the 24-hour diner across the street

i pull the wrapping from my delivery & feel the
the orcas' hunger with their stomachs full of plastic

that we've thrown into their ocean from meals just like this
in the Strait of Gibraltar, they've ripped the rudders

from yachts / sinking four off the Iberian Peninsula this year alone
they understood the assignment the internet internets in response

& who assigned it? this zeitgeist that won't stop whispering,
singing, choreographing the fall of these crumbling empires

its barons seeking solace from fate in underground, luxury bunkers
in Hawai'i or SpaceX launches to Mars / none of them can escape

this timeghost dance / before i feast / i think of how the tsars thought
Bloody Sunday would keep the Russian Revolution at bay

/ before i feast / i look back at the Sunset Diner / from
my window it mirrors *Nighthawks* at the MoMA,

& this conjures memories of my Bratva brothers cleaning
their money in Cézannes & Kinkades that could bend

their cocaine profits to rarefied light / i'll never forget
them telling me in that thick, golden-domed accent

don't call evil to you
let evil do evil

& yet the missiles we send to Yemen, to Gaza, to Jericho, & to Bethlehem
loose innocence from the earth, beckon seductively to figures from our long,

global shadows / our whole nation sexed like what rough beast / riding the
subway i slouch over my phone watching a four-year-old Yemeni boy eat

bomb-barren'd soil & say he'd *rather eat dirt than submit
to this empire* / we've made martyrs of angels

& told ourselves stories about fighting for justice & freedom
that even the most dollar drunk among us no longer truly believe

in this land surrounded by endless wealth for bombs & wasted opulence
i walk past a rum-lit homeless man yelling *fuck you, America* 'til his face

is a burning flag / my tongue brimming with
the kind of magic that won't serve empire

by magic i mean these poems are brewing inside me
& i'm trying to trace their spell in me—in us—

praying they ease time's progression in this incessant country
god, where is this relentless march leading & how

do we make it more of a glide with naps & long
gazes along the way? i'm in the weaving stage

or on it / what i mean is i know our
futures are already interwoven / we're

just slowly finding the thread &
asking it for light / our bodies are the film

capturing the flight of time against them
sounds & words fly past me in Prospect Park:

well the pandemic made time funny for everyone
in truth time was always playing little tricks with us

like a flirty nymph at a river crossing or
a child hiding under the dinner table

the virus just emboldened time to
stop pretending it exists like never before

each passing year an even more glaring
sleight of hand exhausting us further

let this empire fall so we can
have a year of nothing but sleep

let us have a year of nothing but dreams
so we can awaken to this empire falling

this sacred rest that demands cocooning
before the becoming beneath it can wing from us

a time wind to cast us out of the time storm / *el tiempo sin
tiempo* Laura—last syllable pronounced like aura—calls it

or we could also say the true time at times is in timelessness / i
radiate lavender & sandalwood burning smoothly with no fire

Laura & i sat in ceremony with three cups of abuelo
San Pedro filling our hearts & wept with RainCloud

as she prayed over the water & asked it to
wash from us all the time-stained empires

she came all the way from the Andes
with these tears she called forth from us

headdressed in cyan feathers
big enough to lift all of our fears

know that empires always fall my mind
replied / *all of them* & we will be left with

a new sky that was always there waiting for us
sometimes it's easier to see in the clouds

i am in them manifesting a fiercely cozy love on a plane
flying back from the tropics / your head lost in dreams

on my shoulder / beyond the lights of the city
below / i see the horizon falter enough to reveal

itself & i remember you
telling me the night before

in the space before dawn
    i love that we had this liminal-hour exchange

the ecstasy of betrayal & other etymologies

> *Anyone who hasn't experienced the ecstasy of betrayal knows nothing of ecstasy at all.*
>
> Jean Genet

ecstasy comes from the Ancient Greek *ekstasis*
    ek- out of & *-stasis* immobility
        to be or stand outside of oneself,
           or to transcend oneself

    reflecting on all the betrayals
  i move out of myself & into the fire
nothing burns like betrayal
    & what burns the longest are the self-betrayals
        how those first sparks allowed
           the bonfire to rage
                keeping me up at night
                    they roam my nights
                like a pride of star-lions
            nocturnal hunters stalking my dreams
        making them scarce
           we live in a land that betrays
                the earth by forcing its abundance to
                    perform scarcity

America began with betrayals
    sometimes when i walk across it
        i feel this land before its borders through the soles of my feet
a body in America walking over the soil of broken treaties
        i take off my shoes to sieve the sand through my toes
           along the Mississippi Gulf Coast
                i feel the Choctaw walking beneath
                me along the beach
                    & above me in the ocean'd sky
                        tears waving long into the stars

   the betrayals of the Treaty of Dancing Rabbit Creek
     burning a trail through them:
        Aquarius, Aries, Virgo all crying light back down to earth
       stretched wide with night & longing

i'm spinning out all the betrayals lighting my night
   & keeping me from sleep
      i decide to bonfire them to the sky once & for all
        all their lessons & blessings, scattered ashes into
         all the rivers that run through me
           the Mississippi my grandfather swam across
         after school roaring inside me
       on the other side of that mighty river
     the words point back to
   the betrayals woven into the birth of this country
Texas comes from the
   Caddo word *taysha* meaning *friend*

   sometimes all my friends are beyond the body
Babalawo means *father of secrets* in Yoruba
   Baba told me to be careful with my slow-lightning tongue
     everything is listening
       the orixá of fire claims me as his son
        & i better start
         sitting on my throne
       or be crushed beneath it
      shell lips scattered with secrets
     i can't tell you anymore

   are you like me? kept from sleep & dreaming like i dream?
if you give me a secret
   it'll die with me
     but i've given away my secrets
       far too easily in the past
        i swore them to secrecy
         & had to pull myself
         up off the couch at two A.M.

           seven months later
         to set the record straight
      when i overheard my secrets
not just given freely
     but turned away from truth
          you have to watch writers the most with your stories
               (all the writers know what i mean)
                    this is what i mean
              when i say self-betrayals
       usher in
   the wolves

betrayal from the Old French *bitraien*
     to deliver or expose to the power of an enemy
         -traien from the Latin -tradere
            to hand over

         we've handed over seasons & homes
     to hurricanes where i'm from
i gutted sea-logged shotguns in the ninth ward
     after Katrina
        & posted up next to a white limo
            perched on top of the wooden ruins
i'd love to say the winds betrayed us
     but the truth is we betrayed the ocean &
        then betrayed ourselves
             by pretending the get back would never come

        there's something woven into my destiny
     that all the words spoken against me
always get back to me
     even though sometimes i wish i didn't know
        i watch their power fade with every syllable
           even if it happens years in the future
       destiny comes from the Latin *destinare* to
         make firm
     my resolve thickens the blood-gathering

        everything wet will wave from it
i pump a new heart into being
        & ask every heart i've gathered in mine
            not to betray it

        i think of listing the betrayals in a purge
but i don't want to betray my poetry with their presence

poetry is a party line:
        you pick up the phone &
            never know what you're going to hear
                some days it's Whitman singing our oneness
        for every atom belonging to
    me as good belongs to you

i'm told *atom* is from the Greek *atomos* meaning *indivisible*
        but i always thought it was from the Egyptian *aten*
            referring to the *disc of the day*
                the star we all orbit—
            the love in its light & what it reveals
the atom's secret power was invisible for so long
until it opened a new sky in Los Alamos
        i've heard that unleashing that power felt
            like an apocalypse waiting in the wings
                but it's already unveiling itself within us

apocalypse comes from the Greek *apokalyptein*
        apo- meaning *from* & *-kalyptein* meaning *the concealed*
            it is an uncovering of the hidden
        the secrets all coming pouring out like crushed grapes
or broken hearts
        or mushroom clouds
            we've reached the point where we're all looking for
                friends we could apocalypse with:
                    people who would never betray us
                        those who will transcend

                    the night beside us—drinking wine &
                        burning with desires like the stars
                            desire from the Latin *de sidere*
                        meaning *from the stars*
                    when the sun quiets, they illuminate
                all the hunger they've planted inside us
            has grown to a wild garden near-fruiting
        in it the broken-hearted all dance
ecstatically, mushroom,
        & finally explode with light

New York & beyond New York

The verb secrete *can denote either "to hide" or "to release." Both derive from the Latin root of* se-cernere, *to sift apart or to distinguish. Secrets are not buried far from the sacred, etymologically or otherwise, since the value of both lies in their qualities of being set apart, distinguished and defended from the everyday. ... Secrecy may leave hermeneutic space for multiple interpretations and thereby invite pluralism and resistance just as it may occlude and mystify the equal status of human beings and reify hierarchies of power as natural or inevitable. ... Telling a secret converts one form of power, the distinction of possession, into another, an alliance with the secret's new receptor. Eventually, husband turns to wife, or friend turns to friend and says, "Never reveal that I told you this, but ..."*

Paul Christopher Johnson

[we made love on a Brooklyn rooftop under the midsummer sun while Papi[4] watched]

we made love on a Brooklyn rooftop under the midsummer sun
        while Papi watched
        you covered your heartbreak in sass
        even as the sun beat it open
        still you gave me lip pressed through your ache
i tried to reach your heart anyway
        while you rode a beam light into
your belly
        newly conquered time inside you
        you hid it in our footless dance
        but the claves on that Fania vinyl matched a pair of eyes
        spun our way
        so you went even harder & i knew
you couldn't fight the tremble much longer
        felt your glide tremolo, felt you shake,
        you shook the *Lo Mato* beat inside me
        trying to teach me a death, too
        trying to make me an animal sacrifice for ashé
your lovely lips alive like a headless chicken neck still rocking,
        looking to earn my death & reap the magic of its reward
        ghosting you away in a blast of cerulean
        you were up there,
        up, up in the clear before the gathering
        preparing to reign from the sky
                & shout down thunder from clouds
        should it come
                & it did
        with
my eyes closed
        I pulled open the vault of the sky
        revealing us mirrored into each other:

my DNA now reflecting your DNA
        reflecting some rough beast of a new country

---

[4] As he usually introduces himself

    our dreams exchanging dreams,
        waking still dreaming dialogically
            timelines winding together at the base,
        joining the myths & memories of
our youth:

i was a child guiding you through
        corridors of Spanish moss-draped oaks in Audubon Park
        branches with the power to shape light
        roots demanding nectar from darkness
we passed through to the hollow essence of seeds
        the light-compulsion law burning blank
        propelling us blinded into cloud puffs
playing with the double helix words sewn impossibly in their hems
        tearing their immortal secrets open
in the day-dreamed pillow fights of deities
        swallowing war-wounds with sweeps of their eyelashes
it is timelessly us!
        broken bent upward
            carried through the tornadoes of America's
        wet dream wasteland
        Dorothy's now-languid laugh in red poppies
        Papi's stuttering salsa beat love-crooning
        rarefactions of my ancestor's dreams on new soil
            a new soul
                reclining in its own splendor on the stones of
            my forefather's step pyramid
        drawn irrepressibly up our undulating spine
            to the pyramidion apex
the lips of our grind kissed by the sun
        beating down on the spectacle of
        our immortality on a Brooklyn roof
            teasing onlookers with
                glimpses of our flaunted secrets
rituals thrust celestially
        blocking suns
            rapidly oscillating day & night

Phil, my love

Phil, my love
      you left me
not while we were on the ocean floor
      you were not yet ready to share air & i knew
so i squeezed your hand with mine
      among moray eels
the tropical fish
      brighter than the world when it opens to an infant
            &
                  this hallucinogenic pen

we're here again
      apart
            a quiet pulse beneath the ocean's currents

above the surface
      in my bed
            i dreamed i saved a little wolf
                  drowning in a swimming pool
            pumped water from its lungs
                with palms on its belly
            until it breathed again & its tail wagged
              bright

i awoke & you
      showed me a picture of two King Charles Cavaliers
the older immobilized by cancer
      the younger asleep pressed against its chest

but if fire

 still awake
    despite being struck
      hard as a human could hit
       mid-flight
        preparing to use the ground to take off
   225 pounds running 116th downhill
      fist against my jawbone
       in stride
         & how i flew
       but the light switch stayed on
       & i was four paws on the sidewalk into a sprint
        before my full weight could land

all i wanted was a coke to pop from the bodega
  when i left my apartment
  & walked down
  Frederick Douglass Boulevard
    but how could i just ignore her screams?
      she was all alone on a crowded street
    when i ran to her
      i was slipping a cross
       & responding in kind
         & she was escaping him
      before i could speak
     so when i saw four men running towards me
    i thought i could release him from the pavement
     & finally quench my belly-fire
but as her beating had turned to
  his beating would have become mine
    but the light switch stayed on

 even with my teeth wired into a tongue trap
   the light switch stayed on
     before i could speak again
      i was asking you

                        what if within us still: fire
                i'll leave you
                        free to go dark
                                even as you rage against it
                        but if fire
                                here i am again
poking at the embers of a once-blazing bonfire
        on the beach
        once keeping us warm & lit
        & do we build a new structure to burn
        or leave the old one smoldering through sands & sands
                to each timeless core
                        as every star burns time pathways back to us
                        we reach them

that crackhead left the back burners on as his calling card
        stole my 18-karat Egyptian gold bracelet off my dresser
        my mother bought it in Cairo while i warmed her womb
        i was still unraveling the hieroglyphs & what they foretold
        from that moment on it was baseball bats & ruthless eyes
                for anyone burning crills in my hallway
                there's basements along Eighth Ave for that
                        now condos dominate that strip
        but trust me when i tell you:
                we were warriors there decades ago
Jay Black paid me to hold his heroin in between jail stints
        & how do i tell a cop with his gun to my temple
                that he needs a search warrant to enter my place?

quick that steel could cool my brain-fire
        how much time before our fire goes out for good?

        you're always there
on every street
        timeghosts of kissing your eyelids / the corners of your eyes
even waking down Eastern Parkway
        i hug your ghost
even when the lights go out

La Pucelle (Planned Parenthood)

for Joan of Arc

when i wonder how i could ever live my dreams
    when i wonder how we could ever lift ourselves
        from this daily siege
            when i wake up at 4:30
                in the morning on a Saturday
                  so my body can
                      gift space in a crowd
                    who've assembled to assert
              their control of
        a woman's womb
      my body a shield
        for a woman just trying to live her dreams in this siege
    when i wonder when we will rule our own bodies without shame
i remember La Pucelle lifting the siege of Orléans
    in just nine days
        in just nine days
            the timeghosts can gift victory to
                anyone they choose

New York:
the portal to paradise at the end of time

after Simon Verity's *Portal of Paradise*
sculptures at Saint John the Divine Cathedral

*Nuevamente hemos sido testigo de
un once de septiembre bañado en sangre,
donde se viola el derecho más básico
del hombre—el derecho a la vida.*[5]

Pablo Jeria[6]
(May 31st, 1955 - September 11th, 2004)

September 11th, 2001, early afternoon, Harlem:

i came out the door to three ladies sitting on their stoop laughing
    as if time had taken the day off
        eating fried chicken like tomorrow would never begin
            the sun out bright as summer's first promises

walking across Morningside Park
    through grilling & grins,
        basketball & boomboxes blasting *The Blueprint*
            had just come out earlier that day
                the towers still collapsing on repeat
                in my mind
Jay Black ran up on me: *ayo Phil, you heard? this shit is crazy.*
yeah, man, i know! i can't believe this, bro.
yeah, man! this new Jay-Z album is fire!

---

5   Once again we have witnessed a September 11th bathed in blood, where the most basic human right is violated—the right to life.

6   Chilean socialist youth leader persecuted by Pinochet. Over a decade after he passed, I lived in his old New York apartment for a couple of years with his son & wife, Henry & Elaine.

September 11th, 1973, Chile:

Pablo Jeria
is a senior in high school
       a young lion at leisure with freedom in his gaze
             earlier that year the horizon started to
                   burn towards him
                         ignited with Pinochet's hunger for power
                         until this 9/11
                               morning he awakes
                           with the horizon
                 hot in his eyes

President Allende shot himself in the midst of a coup
       & time broke open again,
             running free,
                 unchecked

soon he was captured & taken to Isla Dawson
       pretending the kicks & punches hurt
             to avoid them doing something that actually did
                   but he swears he didn't feel a thing
                         his Mapuche blood runs
                               too hot to feel those beats

even as a prisoner, he raised the spirit of
       the pride, & every beating was a blessing that his organs could
       barely behold, but still he smiled

pacing in captivity for four years
       until four hundred American Visas reached Isla Dawson
             Pablo's name on one of them
                   promising him escape & a new life
                         under a sculpted torch
                               raised above New York Harbor
       hoping for liberty in the nation
             that helped take his birth country's

September 11th, 2002, Harlem:

ayo son, you cuz?
the looping swing that followed missed me by so much
        i died laughing
the follow-up caught my jaw & turned it back towards life
        so we went to war in the middle of 114th
soon he was joined by four more
        the blows were my favorite fireworks
            & i swear i didn't feel a thing
        every shot to my skull burst like a
            star i could see but not touch

fresh ink on my left arm doing its job well:
        the Archangel Michael
            wings just like the sculpture at Saint John the Divine
                protected from all forms of harm down his sword

Brava came & saved me from the bullets meant to follow
        even if it meant walking a full block down 114th
            looking down a gun barrel
                i made it home

the next day i smiled with the sun
        as they asked me in the park:
            ayo Phil, i heard you got jumped last night?
does it look like i got jumped?

September 11th, 2004, Pablo says goodbye:

thirty-one years later to the day:
        all the concentration camp beatings took their final toll

at his funeral, all the Chileans who shared Isla Dawson with him
        wore manes in their mind
             to honor his rule in subjugation
                gifting the space
                      to hear the whispers of future plains

September 11th, 2001, late afternoon, Saint John the Divine:

starburst out of Morningside Park
from the Harlem calm to the Manhattan panic
the light is perfect & the temperature matches my skin
      the same way summer strawberries pair with June,
           men covered in blood & dust or ready to donate
                blood & money line up
                      around the block from Saint Luke's

Saint John the Divine hosts
      the Archangel Michael sculpture
          with a giraffe laid against his breast
              a giant crab claw cutting the entrails of
                  Lucifer's severed head
            the four bases of DNA encircle the scene
              shown as four flames for
            bodies to rise from
a homeless man with deeply gorged, immaculately dark skin
      taps my arm, *i need to show you something*

looking up at the double-arched doorway filled with stone carvings
he points at the slanted underside of saint sculptures, hidden in plain view:
      a twelve-panel progression answering all the big questions of
          what time has carved for us at its end
              when the years melt away to reveal
                  what they've always been hiding

the fourth panel a double helix protruding towards us,
      winding the air within us towards
          evolution
the penultimate panel stops the breath inside us:
      lower Manhattan exploding,
          the twin towers at the forefront of the fire
the final panel reveals the final stage in New York's evolution:
      a quiet Eden with a
          giant ear as its gates
              listening for ecstasy,
                  each pleasure whispering a way forward
                    after this time war finally ends

oceans:
ecosystem & apex

But if such elusive sensations are perceptible to organs other than mine, perhaps what I took to be my own exclusive knowledge is available to everyone, and I have no secret life.

Jean Genet

Thai snake bite

Nobody sings anymore.

Amiri Baraka

i.

there was a road to the beach
        sand blurring its end
        a sky cloudless
                as the ocean's clear reflection,
            wide as a tongue slow
                & relentless
                      in absorbing me
'til I felt that thick power under my foot

at first strike,
        i thought i'd whipped thorns into my leg
            then i saw the two holes
                with blood running from them
i saw a smooth body bright turquoise,
            long into the grass

there was a touk-touk tearing down the street
        that i jumped in front of

& in the one-room clinic where it took me
        i learned there was no antivenom on the island
            as i waved in & out waiting for a speedboat
        under fluorescent lights
that brain melting hit, sweeping
        me upward from myself
            i see a new love coasting on this plane
            not like when i first started falling for you
        i remember that brain bursting
but that was not like this

my blood blessed
        by the tiny rivers the conduits ride between
        the earth & the world right next to it &
        the worlds right next to it
every banded sea krait that glides
        just a vessel to another heart & another & beyond
burn holes to flow through all of them
        all ride rivers of
        neurotoxic elixirs, love, these hemotoxins in my heart
        run through me like
                oceans don't flow
                      they twist & oscillate &
                            drag/pull all the fibers in you

like string fields bend light
orixá, orixá
i bang these stars slow motion out my eyes for you
        irises lost in this tide
                i'm absorbing all the light & everything that comes with it
if you knew what it was like
        being this close to the edge of
                a waterfall
                      beating this hard
                            you wouldn't speak

ii.

                i was ready for the injection
                every initiation is a death
        all the angels bring you back with coconuts

iii.

Oxóssi, Oxúm
these stars that i bang out my palms for you
explode as questions:
what happens when all the little deaths converge into one big death?

                is it the same but grander?
    does the flame flicker in the cosmic socket & not return?
            what do you want to know?
                    all the poets today are afraid to sing stories,
                            i'm just here to
                                    answer sphinx questions,
                                            feel stone give way to
                                                    sand winds

even in paralysis this throb tilts my axis back towards the other pole
        we pretend eros is just in one place
                but it's everywhere
                        woven into all that pulls
death has a magnetism
        that can rob me of my faces & my phrases if i get too close

                these aren't metaphors
                    i'm right here
                        walking the xyst
                            through the black garden

            transmitting across the full bandwidth to anything that can listen
            this is not my place yet
            i have language snaking through double helixes & songs
                    a bursting heart pumping them out into the ocean
                            new freedoms to give / ideas to kill

what is really me starting to perfuse timeless lips
        inexorably wet like when you have no choice but to start a family
i can see the waves of my mother's scream
            when she lost her first son slipping away
                    she can't scream again for her second

death doesn't stand still
        it pulses & storms & diffuses through the walls until
                everything is soaked

    it promises to free that slow
            lightning on rotation
                on your radio every day

i'm not a soothsayer
            but bodies were constructed for these transmissions
                they don't contain them
                      & the avenues of my brain are widening for
                the second lining in the streets that follows the grand boom
        celestial static, then trumpets ride that bass drum

Cecil's long shadow

> for Cecil the lion killed by Walter Palmer,
> an American dentist & big-game trophy hunter,
> with a bow-and-arrow in Zimbabwe

i pumped to private school kids
    & Mount Pleasant crack dealers
        & Boxer Dave
           who broke it down & resold it on Maple Ave
the NCS girls gathered to watch me roll them a spliff &
    talked a gaggle
        to the point
           i couldn't reply
my Ethiopian brother blended cocaine crystals with
    my white widow dust & made a killing along
        Mount Pleasant & Newton
           a killing
              lit brains up like cosmic background radiation
brought to light
when i bought zips from Freddy
    we'd burn blunts subrosa in the woods
        but the handsome Luciferity of
           his features was too bright to
              endure his flawless goatee
                  he brought too much
                      light into this world
                & left behind
            all his limbs charred
he had a sawed-off shotgun & wasn't afraid to use it
i had a sawed-off shotgun & couldn't glance at
    the barrel's black hole sun
        you never know when
           it will illuminate the inside of
                a body

    let me explain to you the politics of the last apex predator,
        elucidate the long shadow cast back over time:
        light hasn't completed the transmutation of a lifespan
            unless the beginning & the end
                shine in new ways beneath it
        like peering into a telescope, looking back
            billions of lightyears to quasars back to the bang
                but a poacher's arrows are
                      silent over Zimbabwe's savanna
    parting Cecil's golden mane,
        piercing his star-skin
            yet it took another night of
                stalking to sear his fate in the sky

            humans love to hunt mortal gods
        before they've reached the peak of their powers

Samuel Sheinbein wrote a recipe for murder
    & avoided extradition from Israel
        Freddy looked like Satan, Samuel said
            he needed to burn, or he would grow too bold
        yes, but he was a charming devil

    some would say the devil got
Samuel Dubose / with his royal mane
    & kind, kingly eyes
        his effortless reign
inflicted a fear that a murderer couldn't contain
        couldn't slow the roll of his car so a cop lit him up
            & here we are in a moon cycle we named Leo
                on the surface of the universe:
            a balloon blowing up to the beat of a silent drum
    blind to its hollow center
left trying to weigh the ghost lives expanding
        the air within us
                Cecil left with all that light to shed down upon us
                    death appears differently beneath it

    new constellations illuminating the last breath of Eric Garner
        & a rage that seems impossible to contain now
            a heat unbearable enough to pull
                blood diamonds from my viscera
                    that is somehow not enough for change
    these days you must let it build & out outrage the outrage
        never waste your anger on the first wave
        for you must have outrage for the outrage
        wait for the second or third to gauge
    the current of the dominant kings & queens of shame-rage
        beneath their royal gaze
        we are all judged differently
        wait for the second or third rage-wave
        lest your voice be swept out to sea
you'll be burned on a stake at the ocean's horizon
        setting with the sun
            watching your psyche search for
                eros
            mimicking Icarus
        & the morning star shooting down from heaven
beneath their royal gaze
        we are all judged differently

    despite the color of my skin
Freddy still took me to Northwest Park
        even though it was called N.W.P. for more reasons than one
the subsonic waves that emanate from any apex predator radiate
        beyond politics & skin
can you feel them all in your hiding,
        where you fled after you felled Cecil,
            Dr. Palmer?
do they shake the earth beneath you while you await
        the ghosts of Magube & his green bombers?
            he made a puppet of a president named Canaan Banana
                & then killed him off with his own sex
        you're a new meal for the king's court
    ignorance is no defense

        now you see why Rhodesian Ridgebacks must gather
                generations of nobility to hunt lions
        now you feel the weight of your desire to
                occupy a space far too large not to swallow you
                        at the exposed peak of an ecosystem like the opening of
                        an orgasm
                              vulnerability is but a matter of attack

        ZANLA troops played Bob Marley cassettes in the bush to
                power the breath of their revolution-balloon
        we played *Chant Down Babylon*
                from his first album after his death
        when we were on E's balcony in Mount Pleasant,
                sometimes the roars of caged lions less than a mile away
                        would catalyze our descent back down from acid trips
                        to alpha stars
                            the weight of apex music
                                  interacting with gravity
                sometimes those roars signaled takeoff
                      when we were at the zoo poking
                        the loudest tourist we could find without
                            glancing in their direction
                                squeezing in vain against the
                                    laughter bursting
                                      from us

they say the universe is expanding like a balloon-drum
        we live on the surface,
                the center just an empty echo,
                        but we know differently now
                                Cecil fell so far to illuminate our cave

who are you to question the exigency of a bicycle?

> for Christopher DeLeon, 28,
> killed by police on June 16th, 2015
> after a verbal dispute over a bicycle,
> written for *Lament for the Dead*

every life has its arc
       & the point past which it can no longer bend
all peoples can only curve so far
all forces echo back at their source in time
       gunshots just do so with ruthless immediacy when you are
            a man with a weapon
like every soul is the source of sound at the center of a great cavern
       we all beat that drum
& if the rhythm moves us into the street
we'll be burning & looting 'til the smoke clears our eyes
       boy they burn
            still with salt but no water left
or we'll be pedaling to a place past the mountains of
       the Visalian horizon
standing like colosseum walls round the blood-sport amphitheater
       why should i die in this dying empire?
who are you to question the exigency of a bicycle in times like these?
       maybe it's time to leave this valley
with its parched aqueducts
       & the incessant whispers of the insatiable foothill Yokuts
growing & growing into a cumulonimbus cloud that won't burst
       from a mother cloud that won't disperse
    to make a clean escape demands one foot
       cascading past the other in cycles
it's the perfect rhythm to ghost dance free of this empirical machinery

i'll be riding that beat for wetness
    or any form of relief
i don't want to say revolution
    they all do & fall prey to its demands

but we can cycle or second line in these streets
        we can second line to salute the sky
                or to pave a pathway to it for our heroes
        we can second line to march this world to its yesterday
            or we can cycle clean through it

i'm back on Cape Cod, eating lobster rolls again

this is America
    & i am here
        deep in you again
            for the first time in this form
Akhenaten's son reborn
        gazing down the rusted railroad tracks
        waiting in an empty train station again
        as the sun starts to set
        a girl with pink dreadlocks
            & *a pig-ear headband*
                enters & makes it just the two of us
        on my way back from Cape Cod
        but still here, still savoring luxurious lobster rolls
            the ocean still with me
            people are really out here being this white
            in all seriousness
            they dream America over & over again
                generation after generation
            it has a pleasant feeling
                like white sharks nibbling at your toes
this young lady is popping the collar of her white polo shirt
        & *she's not even joking*
            wearing white khaki shorts
        an unexpected weapon riding behind her
            hello
you have all this power so use it like never before!
        a bench at the train station is named *NEVERMORE*
            like fucking Poe
        i am back now with new music for you all

you know

i don't know is a shield
you know

beneath that unknowing
your tongue becomes the sword
&
demands a death

we publish come hell & high water

> for my hometown, but especially my uncle,
> Jim Amoss, who was editor-in-chief of
> *The Times-Picayune*, which was one of
> the only sources of accurate information
> about New Orleans in the immediate
> aftermath of Katrina

i.

you're a journalist riding
      to see what she has done to your home
Lake Pontchartrain derided by blushing levees into canals
bursting with what shame can no longer contain
      & now the city must swallow it
you never know what views a bicycle can unveil
from the high ground of the railroad tracks
to your right:
your Creole cottage drowns & gasps on its way underwater
to your left:
survivors with only breath & each other
huddled on the bridge
with no needs right now but to build their
      moments to the keystone of an arc
            over the city curving for
want of the real story
burning for print
in the midst of a deep soak
you're the only witness with a voice loud enough to
reach outside this bathtub of a city
torrents of ink
spilling into the channel

& to the east:
you put down your notebook & your camera
i'm not shooting another picture until i rescue someone you tell yourself
three women & four children about to be carried off by the current
clinging to the last exposed foot of the columns on their porch

the channel now a one-way will stronger than any man
one of the women screaming she'll throw you her child
no you yell
i'll be back

you return in an inflatable boat
    the water is higher now
        the columns fully submerged
            the three women & four children
                no longer there

ii.

now you're us,
the ones who grew up here,
waiting for the
the strongest hurrikin to ever hit
should we evacuate?
should we stay to protect our homes while we send our family to safety?
will we be able to return?
will we return only to be destroyed by the next one?
they're only growing larger
the surface of the ocean is only getting hotter

the temperature rising is just another way to say
time is gathering speed
the August air makes us *slower than a sack of nickels*
    but the heat from the ocean quickens the winds
        our lungs compressed to a new pace
            our voices sky to a new pitch

so the *who dat* chant begins in the troposphere &
    presses the world downward
        until everyone left is under the Superdome's roof
            as it starts to shake & split open

the pecan tree is now draped over our home
    it was peacefully making pralines for generations
        until Katrina came
& left telephone lines hanging from branches like Mardi Gras beads
    over exposed breasts bouncing with the breeze

every day we wait for it:
the salve of the storm thrashing against us again
it's the wait that threatens us

iii.

now you're my uncle
& while you drive a newspaper van into New Orleans
      from Baton Rouge
            to report on your hometown daily
the President says
      there is no way to get in
            like he doesn't command tanks & helicopters

you hear it called a *natural disaster*
      as if we didn't fill the atmosphere with carbon dioxide & methane
            making it hotter than ever before,
      pave the wetlands
            so they can no longer absorb storm surges,
      & let the levees
            fall apart despite your warnings

iv.

you're what the news is calling a *looter*
      breaking into a double gallery along the Esplanade Ridge
            while your ten-year-old son waits in the bushes
                  desperate for fresh water
                        & everything else that sustains life

v.

you're Mayor Ray Nagin:
now get off your asses & let's do something
let's fix the biggest goddamn crisis in the history of this country

vi.

the water is almost at the top of the attic
      so you're beating the ceiling

                stabbing it with your bloodied knuckles
                    grasping its broken pieces
                        to open the roof for breath

vii.

you're Big Chief Monk Boudreaux of the Golden Eagles
        turquoise feathers winging through your sliver of sky
                high above the wind

viii.

you're Jabbar Gibson
just ten days removed from a high-speed chase
        that ended in
                flames & cuffs
commandeering a school bus
        & gliding past police checkpoints
                when they get distracted
        to take sixty people from the Fischer Projects to
                the Astrodome in Houston

ix.

you're a police officer wondering whether your badge means
        anything anymore
                maybe just your gun & ammunition

x.

you're Ronald Madison crossing the Danziger Bridge
        with friends & family
                to search for kin & sweet water
fleeing bullets
     as police
                never a word of warning
        fire at you & everyone you have left
            for the crime of your skin
        you wanted to hate them
                but the twelve-gauge opened your heart from the back first

xi.

you're Malik Rahim building Common Ground in the lower ninth

xii.

you're me swinging a sledgehammer to gut the school
        across the street from Shakespeare Park
        & the Magnolia Projects where you
            balled as a child
you can see your inexhaustible ghost driving
        & finishing with the reverse

        & everywhere you walk
            the dimensions of homes appear so much smaller when
                they're reduced to their foundation
    you can now jump
from where the entrance of your grandparents' house used to be
        to the outline of the dining room
            in one bound

you're in Tremé at the first official second line since she hit
        over two thousand deep in the streets
            dancing & drumming up a thunderstorm under
                the Claiborne underpass
            to let the spirits know it's not time to leave yet
                they will have bodies to play in again

xiii.

you're a city that dances to survive
survival is a dance that never stops inside you
a trance that begins when the sun sets
& the crescent moon water meters disappear underfoot
the city will be chocolate at the end of the day
shining crescent from beneath sea level
getting brighter & darker & lower every day
New Orleans is here for a reason

the city will be chocolate at the end of the day
dirt on your face after being rescued
you must be here for a reason
the city will be chocolate at the end of the day

xiv.

now you are you again
how have you changed?

remembered to forget that i'm god just like you

Let the I be more expansive. Let the I be more flawed.

Reginald Dwayne Betts

infinite duplex with eight gates & a coda:
as you requested, *a written recap of our night*

Even gods have gods.

Nicole Sealey

i → iv → ∞ → in a breath… → ⊕ → in a breath… → ∞ → v → viii

i / viii

remembered to forget that i'm god
in the hungry silence you left me wanting—

        wanting less silence after your hunger leaves
        a picture of you lit up my night

night before you ghosted a picture of you
sucking a thick sausage with slam effect

        sent with slam effect well damn i wrote back
        shot of your lips asking for my hunger

hunger in my lips *what made you think of me?*
largeeee phallic object in my mouth you typed back

        in that *largeeee phallic object* in your mouth
        i can feel my fear a tongue from salvation

what kind of mouth brings salvations & ghosts?
you were god forcing me to remember

ii / vii

remembered to forget that i'm god
& so were you a lip touch away from it

        a lip touch away until i can't hide it
        i can't hide it when you're edging me this long

the longing can't hide on the edge you took me
on the edge you took me past language

        i took you past your edge into song
        teased your song into the fully begging wind

my lips a breath from the pulse of your begging
in a slow drip i taste your want turn to need

        even slower you taste mine turn the same
        fear leaking from the love in your unlocked throat

god link shot between us, the same link you swallowed
& left me godless to remember

iii / vi

even the gods need to write to remember
i want a written recap of our night

        you asked for a written recap of our night
        to remember all of the parts you know well,

you know me so well when you said *i feel like
you have a really good memory for these things*

        my memory once was a perfect film
        asking for an impossible forgetting

impossibly i lit the need in you
on my lounge, 'cross my thigh, you trace a ghost touch

        your ghost touch the last question i left open:
        so you're asking me to write a description

of our night? yess!! goodnight written like an ask
even the gods have gods asking me to write

iv / v

the things you won't say make touch impossible
how could you not say all that is clear to you?

      told me you have no inner dialogue
      is that nebula where all the unsaid burns?

all the unsaid burns nebulas to dreams
& the video you sent me in Signal

      fingers signaling an opening for me
      over & over again until your ache

curved inward aching & back out lavender
lavender L, that's your color in & out

      in & out of my home until you ghosted
      you used to have words in the years you chased

like *i think i'm dizzy from kissing you*
you were still a spin from our years aligning

∞

my body can never open to you
again in this winged way wind traces

      wind traces the back of your throat catches
      sound as it hits & hits its limit

my limit is silence 'til you gift me
a new body for the infinite work

        the infinite work you'll have to do
        to light new nerves, refire limbs & digits

you heat the pulse, the rhythm, the time-stop
of the thing you synecdoche as me

        try & try to synecdoche the whole thing
        into your mouth a night you hunted so long

a night you turned in your mind for years
for years 'fore the dark want opened to the now

        the dark want hanging in the sky-awe
        where you drank stars sky-awe'd & returning

in a breath ...

breaking my form & returning me star-drunk
one day you may come down to me again

        one day you're coming for me again:
        a god i can remember to forget

⊕

                Death is the same in both directions.[7]

[To Coda ⊕ *& then back through the piece in reverse, still reading left-to-right, but moving up the pages, to the beginning.]*

---

7   Hua Xi

self-portrait as past lives

> *Indeed, there are infinite*
> *endings. Or perhaps,*
> *once one begins,*
> *there are only endings.*
>
> Louise Glück

sometimes when i'm alone—
    just the angels & me—
        i remember the other bodies i
            lived in before this one
                breath is how i fly from each one

i pull the tobacco smoke into my lungs
    let streetlamp reflections
        trace the wing-feathers of the
            Saint-Mihiel sculpture
                in the park's rose garden
                    past midnight
    & lay myself across the great expanse of myself
        as all the iterations i used to be still live

in the quiet valleys before inhales

the first time i dropped molly Angela & Mila wrapped
    themselves around me from either side
green-eyed angel A held my left arm stroking it long
    violet-eyed angel M held my right arm fingertip tracing me
something like all the pets at once
i breathed back into a cat i once was
    my jaw jaguar'd in the jungle
        i saw the lines of my jawbones
            mirrored through time
                & finally understood their flex

   these human angels poured themselves over me
     & drenched the floor with my revival
     every new life i described to them as it came:
       of course i placed stones in pyramids
        oh my god of course
          of course Amenhotep IV was my father
          right, clearly, the eyes
         of course i curled, purred deeply in
         the emperor's bed while rose women
         stroked my dark fur the full length
         yes, yes, obviously—
           look at you now

now is a strange & terrifying time for
   the ten-year-old i was alone in the Choctaw forest
     weeping under Spanish moss
       my father's power, our whole way
         undone by manifest destiny
i hold that 1830s child me now
   as the world around us collapses again

again the quietest angel lies under my wings

the first time i got married wasn't the first time
in this life i was seventeen
    & we got married in an alley in Southeast by ourselves
      i wore a silver cape you had sewn for me
        & silver eyeshadow running behind time
   you're even late for your own wedding
     you had a string of pearls from
      your diamond nose ring to your diamond earing
        casting iridescence on your Roma skin
     i bought them all with high school
       drug money in this life

in this life we loved each other out of time
the first time i met you we had already met many times

                we were twins reading each other epic
                        poetry on Crete
                                & finishing each other's sentences
                                i killed your husband when i found out he hit you
                so in our next life together i made sure
                to be the one to marry you
                you died in my arms in a Comanche tent
                        with a spear clean through your ribcage
                                leaking yourself onto me
                                        i went on a killing spree after you passed
                                        & returned home with the blood of
                                                thirteen men on my hands
                when we lived & died in Gansu
                        we needled heart seven & liver three in each other
                                i brewed herbs
                                        to cool your pyrexia
                                                & stayed by your bed
                                                        'til the fire had exhaled

do you remember?

i think this is what you meant when you said
        you trusted me before i told you to
                i warm you up in me like a campfire

we kiss deep as all these lives draw into one
i taste the time-drip
all the water in you leans towards me
        finds its way past anything between us
                like time is
the hunger that pools your spit
spilling all over the god-mind
i sip some prosecco,
pour some cassis
        & make it a kir
i drink some Chianti
i let the grapes' crush run through me / let
your mouth run over me

       the magnetism of other times
            i pull through me into this moment / i pull
love back into me along with
           everyone close enough to bend
                 light into
                        my chest

my heart is a golden thread in Naxos
           labyrinth'd & spinning
           my body minotaur'd like a bright beast
               all my love & all my fire for
                    the unwindings
                        leading to us
                              rocking together
                                  again
                            but in this new way
                     in this new life

along the Pacific
        coast almost tasting the equator
            in San Juan del Sur
i lay down   slowly   sliding down the long   stretch of   you
       past you
           beyond your limit   we laid back   away from each other
               forming two polarized magnets
                   interlocked at our center
                       upper thighs under upper
                            thighs
                         heads opposite each other
                             both sky-facing
       like earth's axis leaning
           west / the whole tilt
               aching north to south & back
i raised a rhythmic tide deep in you
       until the sea sprayed from you
              my eyelashes   my lips   my chest   some past life
            all drenched,
                all drowning in you

recovering my body

Light enters a cathedral the way persuasion fills a body.

Carl Phillips

spell to name the spell

after Natalie Diaz

let me call my anxiety, the still before the breath that begins it all
let me call this coming poem, a spell
      to finally send my life in motion through my limbs

let my lips speak my words now;
      tease new lips before my tongue teases them further;
           semicolon the most erotic lean between singing lips
          pull the crave from the cells that need it most;
                i burn the quiet into this moment,
                      lightning trails for future music

self-portrait recovering my body:
spell to bring the body back

for all the survivors

i.

i hold my sex
    follow an amethyst vein the length
        & let it pulse with the pace of
            all the hunts it's survived
  how it's been stalked by hungry ghosts,
    prized like lion manes,
        endured a downpour of restlessness,
            escaped the rhythm of my grasp

how i've lived this long with a body that keeps leaving me
    is a miracle of spirit
        a quiet wind of words without breath
            i feel the stigma start to touch me
                my heavy stamen rising with it

pleasure in my pleasure body waiting like pollen thickening

i watch the flowers wave desire out
    the window of my train upstate
fog thick & rough like cat tongue over the Hudson
    the river & the clouds nearly one
on the railroad tracks i ride a line between them:
    my body obfuscated on one side
        & immutable on the other
these are the years i stay ageless
    time moves clean through me
        but leaves no marks

when the river warms the fog back to vapor
    i see my physical form on the horizon
        this body is mine
            but so distant from me

it keeps the score
    recounting to me all the moments
        that created space between us
           still raging at all the times
              i let it be taken from me

ii.

let me call this window that gazes into me as i write,
    a solitude on display,
        a theater of solitude,
           a spotlight into my quiet,
              a body leaving solitude
                  & tasting new light

have you ever been alone inside bodies?
    i'm unbounded, hourless even writing
        a comma is a slow ripple

iii.

my body is a poem that can recite itself into presence
    not just for the ars poetica of naming poems spells
        but the ars poetica of burning conceits into the air
           until they rearrange the stars within ourselves

iv.

listen, i am god just like you
it's time to wake up hot in the god-link
let your rage burn the fear that kindles shame

feel your fingers print music
        onto everything you touch
gaze upon your own reflection
        & cast rose petals over everything in sight
adorning yourself in new vows
slow time to a drawl in your mouth & repeat after me:

on the other side of the resistance,
        somewhere in the flowers
                i have a body with no age
                        every motion its way
                                builds the moon's pull in me
                        every desire i hold
                waves into my bay
        the sky is just a
mirror of the sea

rise from a bed of lavender,
        hyacinth, phacelia in all their cycles
                scattered across your dreams
                        all the purple you've been waiting on
                              widening your jaw
                                      to its limit, aperture agape
                              the sound free-flowing
                    from your throat
                will lead you to it
        somewhere in the flowers
you have a body with no age

poems as spells

*Adorn yourselves, dance, laugh—I'll never be able to throw
Love out the window.*

Arthur Rimbuad (translated by John Ashberry)

naming cats

my parents were living on the corner of Saint Philip & Royal
    when my mom got pregnant with me
        they were going to name me Levin
            after Tolstoy's mirrored creation
    but just before it was too late,
my uncle called:
        you're not naming cats
            & i ended up Philip

my cat died in my arms this Easter
    he woke me up that morning
        to let me know today was
            the day for him to go
    just like he ran up on me
    mid-*Talk Facts* in my headphones
& damn near tripped me as i turned onto my block
    to make it clear
        that it was time for
            me to take him home

i share these stories just to say:
    somehow
        even free to choose new fates
            we're all practicing
                the things that have already happened

we kissed for the first time last week
    like we knew we would
        after months of build
            & we touched like a time-tear
                just starting to rip

when you leaned in for more
        i pulled away
                to tease you
                        & melt minutes to something smoother

when i leaned in
        you pulled away
                to tell me you're getting your eggs frozen this year

you've been staring at the alien objects on my altar ever since
        eyes light & clear into mine:
                how many spells have been cast in this apartment?

thinking of the brain-whip of winds & snuff you'd never heard of
        marked with your name before i'd heard it
                more than fifty
    i reply
                because *hundreds* would sound terrifying
                & spells work best in the calm after the fear / or the bliss
                before it begins to wave

we can make anything we want
we have the sparks to burst into new worlds

just don't wear out the magic with the trying
        i whisper to myself
            in my sleep
                i can line an arrow through
                      the eye of the time storm,
                            light a new star to a concert,
                                heat our lip-quiet to
                                    a quiver:

        we can name ourselves anything we choose

letter to my godson Kaimel
on his third birthday

Kaimel
    let me tell you a love story
        my father used to read me Greek & Egyptian myths before bed
            one day i'll do the same with mine
    let me tell you a love story & what i know of god & the gods &
love & of being your godfather

love is so close, ahijado
    it's on the tip of my tongue
        edging closer to speech
            i know my beloved feels it coming
                i'm a breath from ready now
        a dandelion puff one sway from seed-burst
            this is how love spreads itself

at your third birthday party
we rode the lion on the carousel together
you didn't want me to put you down
    little lion cub with paws over my shoulders
your sister wrapped herself around my neck
    you lil phony
        your mother tells her
            now she wanna be sweet
    her head on my shoulder
        a future body letting me feel what love
            will bring me for just a moment
Liz facetimes Shaquana & sees me beside her
what's up, Phil? your hair looks good

what can i tell you about your godmother?

Liz looked me up & down at your baby shower:
> *big padrino energy*
>> drip like the bottle pop leaning down the bottom lip
>> we drank so much prosecco in the project hallways
>> celebrating you, leãozinho
>>> the whole day champagne'd to a brain bubble
>> we had the Brownsville Houses lit to a summer solstice
>> i lit a spliff
>>> & toasted you with smoke
>>>> *i love you already, bb boi*
>>>>> more puffs out the tongue gate
>>>> as i dance to the *Leg Over* beat from the bluetooth
>> L's a grin rising
>>> *ayo godfather pull up*
>>>> we were suns bursting for
>>>>> you were almost here

i was ablaze & out-of-body
watching two shorties fight out front
> hair in teeth
> hands in ripped shirts
>> breasts in the wind—

the strength of the resistance
> is always weaker than the power
>> of the bliss on the other side of it
>>> don't wait 'til death to slide into it

i can taste heaven splash back from not my beloved's mouth
> she's beside me whining for more
>> & the whining is getting to me
> making me pool bigger
>> i gather the holy sea on my fingertip
>>> brine the tip of her tongue
>> i've been deep in the prayer trying to hold my seed
>>> i'm saving the wave-break for my beloved
>>> *everything you do is perfect she tells me*
>>> *how do you always know exactly what to do?*

        but she is not my beloved so how perfect could i be?
           i pull her hair back tilting her head to the sky
            & remember my love
                i walked out of heaven for
        the thing we both keep turning from
        i have a religious devotion to hunger
        i marvel at my will power
           knowing will will only carry me so far
              it will take me to the edge of
        the surf
        but it can't make the ocean wave
    Misha says your middle name is Will for a reason
        after i tell her the story of your birth

i was deep in the prayer until dawn that night

our urge to communicate is god's
    the words seem impossible until they come
how the same thing that's just a trace on the horizon of possibility
    swells large & undeniable in the back of your beloved's throat
when its time has finally come
leãozinho, let me tell you a few things:
    sometimes *i don't know* is brave
        & sometimes it's cowardice
            know the difference by seeking why you chose it
be careful whom you take advice from
    most people mean well
        but they're just seeding you with their fears imagining
            that they're protecting you
      & fear always whispers that it will keep you safe if you
        just hold it tight forever
            until it births itself before you

i reentered the city the day before you were born
i was driving through Jersey in my father's car staring at
    the New York skyline when
        Shaquana told me L had gotten locked up

                        on a nonsense parole violation
i know you saw that from above & didn't wanna come
            your pops on the island
                    mom's water about to break
                            the world in a pandemic
                                    i don't blame you

at the moment you came into this world
            i had lips on me
                    when Liz texted me *he hasn't cried yet*
            there are bunch of doctors around him
                    & she sent me a pic of you surrounded by blue scrubs
                            clearing out his airways
i had practiced for this, Kaimel
i cleared my space
            asked the love on top of me to let me breathe bigger
                    i reached out to every angel, every ancestor i knew
                            & they came
                                    i asked them to go help you
                    but they said i had to go myself
                            i felt wings lift off my back
                    i entered lightning slow enough to ride
                            you told me
                                    you didn't know if
                    you wanted to come into this mess
                            it is a hot mess out here
                                    July 8th, 2020
                                    COVID choking the life from bodies
                    Black bodies still being choked for breathing
            your father locked in a cell inhaling jail air
                    lord i understood
                    but i vibrated joy for you anyway
                    every cell shook like heaven for you
                    i promised you
                            i would be there with you for
                                    every ceremony
                                            either in body or spirit

        i told you you were going to live a joyful life
          that you would be
            so happy you were born
              you said *yes*
       & Liz texted me that you had started to breathe
Shaquana told me it took fifteen minutes
    for oxygen to enter your lungs
        five days later they put me on facetime
          with you from NICU
            they say infants can't smile
              but you were
                grinning ear to ear

listen more & listen more to what i can tell you, ahijado
learn from my stories
listen for the songs inside the chaos
    your sky-piercing shriek a search for new frequency
but sometimes you just need to sit back & watch it all perform for you

i've married perfection & the cost was my beloved
    like walking away from someone who really loves you
    whom you really love
    again
    like, wait, don't go
    they don't love you like i love you

the Abrahamic followers
    say god is perfect
        we're all just trying & failing to be like him
that's a wild game for a narcissist to dream up
    sitting in the clouds & punishing
        them all for not being more like him until they die
no, it's all inside us
    every angel, every demon,
       & when we open enough, we become them
god is just an everywhere ghost needing connection so badly
    that atoms bond to other atoms & form molecules

    even when they split
      the spooky action brings the love back to life
until then i write to survive
  i sing to survive
    i call on the heavens to survive
      i protect you to survive

tomorrow i will know more
  & surrender other knowings
    & this is how you get to the essence of things

what can i tell you about your father?

i met L in Inwood park
  flying off some boomers & asked to drive his go kart
    round the baseball diamond
      we hung 'til sunrise
    & got lit in the Dyckman Projects with Chaz (R.I.P.)
      & Devon
        & burned in Harlem
    he got knocked for the Nina with priors
      & got eight to ten
    i put money on his books every season
he wrote me from Clinton, from Upstate, from Sing Sing
  so many letters, Kaimel
    every one ending *i love you like cooked food*
i visited him on Riker's
    they yelled at me 'cross the courtyard
      Dude, where's your car?
  i wish you knew how fucking funny that is
L said he'd beat their ass if he found out who said that
  he broke a CO's jaw
    & got sent to solitary
      right before he went
  he left me a voicemail:
    ayo Phil, they gave me three months in the box
     that's nothing

      i do that standing on my head
       it's a small thing to a giant
   that was his favorite phrase for years
    he doesn't say it as much anymore
  but i miss him dismissing the world like a lion tail to a fly
   i have stories i can't tell you here
    but we go see people
      & we'd never let anything happen to you
       i want to be able to tell you
     like i can hold off death
   maybe at times
   but i am there with you for every ceremony
leather jacketed & black tied for your grandfather's funeral
   he was a thunderstorm drummer with perfect pocket
     his rhythms beat in you, pocket heartbreaker

what i can tell you about your mother?

Shaquana's a slow burn
   menthol out the window of her car
    get the fuck out the road
     no tolerance for performance
     woman
we're vibing to Roddy Rich *i ain't tryna die
young* over the Kosciuszko Bridge
that's a beautiful bridge she says to me
   it's the first time i've heard her say the word *beautiful*
i ask her where she found your name
   it was just in my head she tells me
she got a cool fire on her head
   & i ease it when i can
the price of diapers these days is wild
a couple hundred to send boxes to your house
thank you for everything you do for these kids
   i know she's serious
     but i wanna laugh

       like she's not spending day & night for you
    Kaimel, your mother got a tongue with no remorse
      but she gives her life to care for you & Paris

i think they may have loved each other
now they say things about each other i can't repeat
    not even in this poem
Shaquana holds up a picture of you
   tell me that ain't L's face
when i say i want to see people
    i mean it in every way
      i know they feel rejected when i still don't call
this one body needs one home
     i want to hold my beloved's hand while she gives birth to our child

what can i tell you about your grandma?
she rang in your birth with us in Brownsville
    & she loves you fiercely
      i'll tell you of the first night i met a different abuela
      the night that prepared me to
       welcome you to this world

i drank three cups of the Colombian brew & called in my guides

Yeshua
    flying in the shape of a cross
      emanating rainbow fire breathing
       sudden bloom from seed
        & scorched earth

Archangel Michael with his sword flaming blue
    came to me more & more massive
      & turning towards deep sea purple
       he filled me with that light
         & all the sex thoughts divine & pulsing
i was rock hard in ceremony
    the taste of Colombia still a pulse on
my tongue talking with a winged reflection telling me:

i am you & you are me
   no
i am you & you are me
    yes, we are all one
no, i am you & you are me

i didn't want to hear it
   lord that message scared me
      but i needed that message to know how to talk to you

Oxóssi came & danced with me
   laughing like a big brother
     oke-aro
       oke, oke, oke-aro through the shoulders

maybe we create these gods & angels
   because knowing all that power is
     in us is too terrifying at first

the night you were born we were deep in the prayer 'til dawn
   reminding you of who you are

& in it, i remembered, too

we were angels' wings spreading into the infinite side by side
we were lions rubbing manes in the Sabi Sands
all these lives we've lived & still time has yet to touch us

know this: time is just a trick to allow us the joy of repetition

& you will live a life of unspeakable joy
   joy building upon joy like waves catching bigger waves forever
     crashing & waving again still higher
       the wind will not fail you, Kaimel

& you will always return to joy & knowing again in the end
   just as i do, you will always see it all

        maybe not when you want to
          but when it's time to

repeat after me:
    i direct the air within the air
        i light the colors inside their reflections
            every day a banquet is laid before me
                & i choose the lips most open to mine

repeat after me:
            i live a life of infinite joy

City of Gods

i.   enter

at the heart of every truly epic party
    is sleep
        & the promise of
            home

      up the dream
          rising the bifurcated staircase
              helmed by a many-limbed love
                free of gender
            whole mouth fuchsia
          headdress high as molly
     mirroring back everything
         you need to leave behind to enter

ii.   grace

    the grace you give me
    the grace i give you
    gets us through the gates
    every Halloween is a new beast begging birth

    we can only enter this world unarmored
    all the shields: the stories, the timelines,
        the people keeping us safe from paradise
    they can't enter here
    even if you yell at me for them
    they're not my fault or yours
    the time for blame is over
    the time to be brave is now
    Oxóssi this night
    for us god was twice a hunter
    only those who choose to be
        prey point fingers outside themselves
    the holy shed
        their shields, say their farewells, &
            enter the air hollow'd by the arrow

    could we be the ones who adorn
        our headdresses with each other's flaws
            & laugh at their armor as it falls away
                like mad cicadas

    sometimes you have to surrender knowing,
        unknow & live unburdened,
            to let the knowing come to you again in its time

    like every dance

    heaven is a vibration
    when you vibrate with it
    it always comes to you
        like a properly ignored cat
            i tease its lack 'til it's at my toes again

iii.   **universe**

spiritual teachers walk around saying the whole universe is within
        but, fuck, have you really witnessed it?
                when the absence of someone is also a presence
try a new room
        with a swing band proposing *o when the saints*

everything winged yet earthbound is here marching
        under godly lights in this ark
                we're all dancing around the clown fish'd aquarium

we need the whole story here with us to
        unveil what could be
so i gather all the moments you leave out
        in your retelling
                & decorate the ballroom with them:
                        they're in the candle-bulb's reflection
                              the reverb of the synths
                                      the final note of my laugh
                                              still caught in the
                                                      delay
                              & here you are finding them

silver plates of strawberries
teasing your tongue
oh hushing the hunger-dream

iv.   **dance**

quick before the time need returns
Allaha a new dance between us
miracle my step back in sync with yours
spin us back round beside the river long
sunset us into a new cuadrado

cumbia our chests   for just one clave   & another   & another

we are always syncopated

the angels are always dancing
we're dancing
we are the angels
        in this unstoppable way
                i can't unhalo my heart for you
        its wings beat a light path for you
            & i'm walking it with or without you
            with or without you
                we're in this light together
i can't unrhythm the night of you
        drum burnt of seashell,
            regret a lie washed from the waves
                the whole ocean costumed for us tonight
                adorned with this love god poured into my skull-less head

i can feel it unwind my brain
        relieve strength from my limbs
            i hang into the sky ceiling below
                from wedding cake balconies
my love like new wine leaking
my heaviest curl asking all kinds of wherefores
& cussed back at
the most Romeo motherfucker i've ever seen
        but this heart-stop leaves my face unRomeo'd while i'm wordless
            only to Romeo my expression
                further for the true start of our story

this dance floor: so many prayers for love
    in conversation
        with what you seek at all times
            let's step into a quieter space & become clear

v.   marriage

    lounging behind translucent drapes
    i need someone brave enough
          to celebrate this moment of union
                with abandon
                      here in this gauzy,
                            infinity-pillowed refuge
                                  spoiling each other to Elysium
                                  with words
                                  with every touch
                                  with every possible adoration

            (i kiss the violet around your eyes
            that's not there but colors what is)

    for anything less than that
          don't even bother glancing my way
                or speaking my name
                      leave me hung heavy with prophecy
                            heart hanging root-low
voice bass'd / screw'd / moody'd
          body ecstatic & sweating you out

in our freedom we're rushed by Victorian actors
          with an altar & a ring asking us to perform a proposal
                the whole crowd cheering,
                      snapping pics, & thinking it's real
                            but even in this staged ritual & vows
                                time comes undone in me

the whole event stilled
          all the cats are around my fingers now & i'm
              maned, clawed, whisker'd along with them,
                  lions circling my index
                  i'm lying married amongst them, being them
                      asking for nothing
                            while they feline towards me
                      always wanting more from me

sleeping a storm through us
        shepherding hurricanes through delta waves
                cell phones still don't show up in our dreams
                because they're just training wheels for telepathy
                & we're already talking silently from afar

in this godly way
        on the other side of the heartbreak
            everything is done for me

in a gush of hands
        weeping upward for me
            in this way, too,
                my heart
                      is quiet, purring
softly vibrating a beast bold enough to bend cathedral light

        the light that's already entered
            persuasive enough to keep persisting
                deep / deeply tasting the unpurred parts of you

        chandeliers spilling refractions a silent slit to
        illuminating all the ways
            in which we are
                a church forming in each molecule
                    blessing the brain last

all the tears flowing upstream
        god like a tiny water nymph playing in them
            leaving me wanting for nothing
                the massive magnetic vortex in
                    the center of my chest
                pulls everything to me
            like my heart is
        my own heart's waiter
i am brought everything

in one vow you are invited to
        every celebratory moment in my timeline
            i think this is what marriage really means
                in every past, present, future triumph
                we are bound & set free

vi.   **moonlight**

how many times can you hear
    i love you in one night
        before the four chambers flood?
      depends,
      but with the full moon counting,
          somewhere between eighty-eight
              & one hundred eleven
      am i in a movie? the way you're glittering under the moon
      the moonlight loves
          showing trailers for coming nights

raised up,
    swaying,
        hooded over me like a cobra
Wadjet from above
    directing your mouth at mine with so much fury
      twisting lips to the high hats
          fluttering dragonfly wings at each other
              every motion ferry'd between us
                  & not needing completion
the kind of dance that answers the question of what to do with
    all the knowings whose time hasn't come yet
      i've buried them in the air for you to find
        in the moment you're finally ready
          to breathe again,
        not a breath for escape or survival or relief
      but breathe within the body's bliss one more time
it's happening now
    awning'd under the stilted man-creature's silver eyelashes
      this is a place where you can't lie to your body any longer
        the heart finally quiets the mind
            & swallows all the half-sunken myths
      everything is here now
      thick & undeniable
        but spread out through time
      a precious few moments are crowned *finally*

my crown slants
        left undoes the
                shine in you
                      only to redo it
                              brighter & bigger &
                                      for good this time
                                              pulls us into
                                      a courtyard

vii.   **gloria**

watching an a cappella medieval gloria
glide past us
handing chocolate shrooms to all my friends
posted up on a stone fountain
god: a sprite rising from it
raising the hair on the back of my neck
      with a breath
            stealing psilocybin from my palm
                    & glances
                         leaving me

eye to eye with god
promises beyond promises
i will receive you or
      someone who choirs my heart it wasn't you
            my bliss is new Eden, now kingdom, angel-sealed
& in this knowing i remember how thorough /
      how thick / how quiet / how thorough /
            how thick / how loud / how heart-stilled /
                  how heart-drunk
            i can be after a fall

viii.   **afters**

the courtyard comes nightly
spilling into a flower garden with its own light
      we have to be the happiest, most enthusiastic visitors
           to ever enter this garden you burst
                most profane i add
    but in the roses
        there's bumblebees wearing fur throws
            furthermore
                the leather bike gang bumblebees are really
                    living in that pollen

i understand now why you wouldn't want to reopen that door
    this grief is an initiation,
        a garden laughing wildly in reverse
            & when you leave don't
                write the joy out of the flowers
                    even with too many colors to
                        gaze back upon

ix.   **home**

    the music just a pulse beneath us now
    the whole world our bed
    lying on my chest
    asking *why are you so cozy?*
       knowing the answer is you're finally home
           it's so obvious now
    come home, Odysseus
    come home, Odysseus
    i tell myself
         like everyone is a mirror
              all of existence is me pushed out
especially tonight
what good is love if it can't flow
       through pride & fear & dare to begin again
          spill from fresh anger squeezed hot &
              unfed, your legs grip my left thigh
i had to ask for the fan
      the way your hunger sweat through the room
          the same way resistance is just a door to a deeper desire
    & fear is just a mask for something new & waiting for
        first breath
            anger is just
               a Cerberus guarding
                   something much bigger &
                      more mysterious
i know i can sing it to dreams
      the way you've Orpheus'd my throat
        free of sound
           in your sleep
               felt your body shake & shake
          the whole underworld
        shaking on my thigh
            the old folks on porches say *hotter than Hades*
               but they don't know this kind of blaze
        if we can't alchemize this once eternal heat,

                    transmute this bass into a whirling dervish
                            we would've failed
                                        at something else anyway
                                & we were never meant for this city
                        the gods here don't fail at anything
                    they just leave hints of their return
on your dining table,
        my windowsill,
                floating
                            in the sky of
                                    our one shared mind
                                            as i wake & leave

x.   left

you left yourself all over my left thigh, my glance, my return
all this glitter is coating the morning in a staying way
        in a staying way
reflecting a night magnified & split into infinite specks
                in this light it's so easy to see what everyone else is avoiding
                        until the mirror reveals a rager in my own belly
                              a blind eye cast over it

when i left i felt you finally let yourself think of me

xi.   **even**

even stilled & thought finished
the celebration returns in waves
in this way, heaven materializes
        if you stare at it knowingly
                the way everyone missing
                        become bodies again
                                when set free

even   ghosts

even   gods

the spirits who feast with us

My final prayer:
O my body, always make me a man who questions!

Frantz Fanon

duplex with four gates for Rex:
prayers to a new cat god passing in my arms on Easter Sunday

my heart is at its limit, Rex, listen:
can you hear its murmurs, its lost whispers?

    your ghost whiskers murmuring saints on my chest
    prayers for my heart pulsing questions

the time question pulses to a broken count
chambers asking what now of our home, Rex?

    i gave you a home, a pillow on my bed
    your eyes level with mine, wide & unblinking

wide awake leveling clouds to a smoke
i was ten puffs to the sky where you loomed

    purring wise in the sky puffs: *there's a new way*
    you broke my stride vibrating *a new way home*

ran onto my block, heart vibrating ice
the winter chill caught in your chest

    the January chill blocked by my headphones
    Bronx drill blasting: *even my abuela knows that*

abuela knows your softness despite the streets
leaving your heart pierced, martyred, aflame,

    broken & Catholic as my grand Mere
    i warmed you every way i knew how

every warming a soft knowing
every week a new vet bill & healing

        every night you hummed a healing to me
        your body overflowing with gratitude

grateful to not be dying cold & alone
on a street that doesn't know your name

        now my ancestors know your name
        lamping on my couch beneath my second great's frame

my second great's frame carried on a throne
in the Rex parade along my childhood street

        my childhood street turns for a prince's dance
        to a pirouette for the King of Rex

the King of Rex spinning a storm of want
Rex, you prepared me for my next love

        prepared my next home in the sky-love
        colors wanting nothing, brushing sky with Mere

soaked in watercolors for want of nothing
i know she's sunned your fur with Christ hues

        in the sunset your eyes painted in Christ hues
        when every storm passes, Rex is risen

Rex rose & woke me storming at the mouth
Easter strikes again, again my dreams give to

        your mouth foaming dreams in the Easter sun
        telling me it was time—you're dreaming of another home

perched on my thigh at the vet dreaming time's end
that injection shut the lights off lightning quick

        that lightning stilled your heart to a light
        left me with your lifeless body in my arms

your body suddenly still to my touch
skin whispering to you: *live again, lil bear*

        lil bear, my pocket lion, heart whisperer
        we are still timeless before the dream-break,

but the dream-break arrives, says I must wake &
pull myself from the timelessness again

        from the timelessness, my heart seeks your meter
        Rex, listen to my heart's limit, crown its break

Juchereau Oxóssi SaintDenis / Maria Oxúm Sánchez

for my ancestors & orixás

because you came to me while i was standing on a hill
    overlooking the favela
        Cidade Nova
    new city in the capital of the world: Salvador, Bahia
        & made time reveal itself as the greatest joke of all
    i laughed at myself for pretending to be in it

because you came to me as a snake & filled my veins with love
    & then
        dropped sweet-
            water through the IV
                while i waited for the winner of
                the race between the helicopter & the speed boat
        you initiated me in the ICU of Bangkok
            Hospital-Koh Samui branch in the midst of
    paralysis Maria pumped my heart, while
Juchereau pumped my liver
for your beauty, i was breathed
i was breathed because you came to me in the Panamanian jungle
    rusted barb wire in my foot
        we watched drunken group bullfighting in the waiting room
            debating the worst of
                the sins: the sport or the nurse's choice of show
    some people claim to have had imaginary friends
        i have no idea what that would be like

because poems defeat time, but it's already dead

because you must be beautiful while you hunt
    or why would you even bother

because you told the Babalawo i was a worthy initiate
    & showed him my ancestors practicing as he does

because we always come together

despite my fear
my lifelong fear that only became clear
    upon seeing the request in your faces
        i let you in my body
        i let you in

i got back from Bahia (all the saudades)

i got back from Bahia
        swarms of spirits knocking on my nights
                shivers of ghost-sharks circling
the saudades are stalking
        won't leave
        won't let me be

i stood outside the terreiro
        overlooking the hills of Cidade Nova
                the time-joke: a fog finally lifting
                        favela hut tin walls coming apart at the corners
i count their cracks as i count the beads in my necklaces
        for whom they represent
                oh to finally know who they are
        the confusion of past moments distilling
                to a single, clear kindness
        i just want to gift it to you
                this is exactly where i need to be
                where i was led

how did the Babalawo know my ancestors practiced as he did?
how did he pick me from the chanting crowd?
        fighting the eye roll back to my brain
                & the loss of control
                        stepping out moon-drunk & trying to still the spin
        he knew exactly what it meant
                he knew exactly what i needed to know
& how did he know my brother was still above me watching
                & when i learned their names!
        that they had always been there for me

back in my bedroom
        every nerve ending antenna fully extended
                protecting against the inevitable loss

　　　　　　i turned the lights on as a momentary shield
　　　　　　　　　　reached for more armor:
　　　　　　　　　　repeated the rhythms Neguinho do Samba
　　　　　　　　　　　　　beat for me
　　　　　　　　　　when i was his chosen pupil
　　　　　　　　　　receiving invitations to perform with Olodum
　　　　　　　　　　　　　in Pelourinho
　　　　　　　　　　remembered that gatinha Rose dressed in all white &
　　　　　　　　　　impossibly choosing me for the New Year
　　　　　　　　　　　　　drank from my maté gourd
　　　　　　　　　　all to escape sleep
　　　　　　but i had burned all my oil on the last thirty-six nights
i couldn't hide from what was waiting for me in the dark any longer
　　　　　　so they came
　　　　　　　　　　flashing between my brain-screen & my eye
　　　　　　　　　　　　　light-blinding my vision
　　　　　　　　　　　　　　　　grasping at my breath
　　　　　　　　　　　　　　　　　　　& then the music rolled in
　　　　　　　　　　　　　　　　　　　　　clean & high
　　　　　　　　　　　　a childhood song my brother played for me
　　　　　　　　　　　　o won't you help to sing ...

& the next morning
　　　　　　the paper already sprawled out on the dining room table
　　　　　　　　　　Style section of *The Washington Post* laid out on top
　　　　　　　　　　　　in honor of his birthday:
　　　　　　　　　　　　Celebrating Marley's Ghost

& how i wait for you
& how i wait for the moment when time can melt away
　　　　　to just us again
& i'm here holding all the saudades at once
　　　　　(oh my i miss you)
　　　　　　　　　　all the saudades

how are the laddies?

> for my grandfather

chess is a negotiation with a future
    that might already be decided
a battle of dueling prophets
    to command space for with it comes time
        its flow & its ghosts
the zeitgeists that humble every jagged, protruding desire
    smooth every stone
but his movements were frictionless
even with his massive mind riding the full length of
every future wave around him
    reaching even past the crash
his movements were frictionless
so time filled him up & kept flowing
& he threw the tennis ball for Laska again & again
& he asked *how are the laddies?* again & again
& held the great expanse of himself lightly on the piano keys
    still listening
        for the sounds that allow for the locating of Lilith
        in the screech owl night
            that at last comes in threes
        when the chess future finally renegotiates with space
        to align the timeghosts around him

land back on Tchoupitoulas[8]
(no one else can bring my music)

i burn an L gliding down Tchoupitoulas
    smoke trails linger on the past
        even if the Gulf rises & swallows
            the whole city to the hilt
                these streets can't be unnamed
        like spells bound to the wind beneath the wind—
            the wind that drives the wind & makes it howl

abandoned & abandoned & abandoned again
    in quiet ways like the Chapitoulas, in more ways like the wind, i
        still have breath & a voice
        still i can cascade a cataclysm from the clouds
            it's always raining when i leave New Orleans

let me show you the power of these ancient words
    krewe of Choctaw, krewe of Tchefuncte
        i can shout down heaven from a float
        sha the banter we on
        where y'at on Choctaw, Caddo land?
            dancing on broken-treaty'd concrete
                oak roots pumped thick through the sidewalk
                    arcing justice into the second line

you can't speak of Louisiana's birth
without the Natchitoches words
    rolling lip-shaped breath into the mist
        i heard my seventh great calm the air in ceremony
            drink the second cup
                do what you came to do

---

8   Tchoupitoulas St—named for the Chapitoulas tribe, who were one of the original inhabitants of the land that is now New Orleans.

        Chief Big Leg, bless the medicine chalice
            before i drink again
                one thing about me
                    my ancestors don't play about me
                        you can test the waters
                            & be swept out to sea
                      like the French Navy trying to
              hold onto Saint-Domingue
            your stories & technology won't protect you

i was thinking about the stories
            people must tell themselves to persist in their way
                & how the stories keep them from seeing
                    what's already on its way back from the sky
                    keep them from
                          rolling back the time curtain
                    & hearing the return
                sung into the names
            they say every day
        & how they'll define
their future

what do you really know about these Tchoupitoulas blocks?
yeah, i know you know F & M Patio Bar at Lyons
            where we used to have the Franklin reunions
                whiskey-deep in spirits & unaware
drunk before the sunset
            fully-dressed oyster po' boys at Domelise's
                demanding our full attention
we'll destroy anything in our way to get them
the Tchoup Shop's windows smashed for the ATM once again
            what else did they expect?

côte des Chapitoulas
        some history books say the tribe is now extinct
but can't you taste the swell?

        hear heaven's shell start to crack
            in a triplet tap dance on the cobblestone
                named for those who live by the river

god how they love the flow &
    how they rule this city
        in the dusted brass of Frenchman,
            the Quarter,
                Tremé,
                      i hear the last laugh of a fate
                decided by the disappeared
            my head bowed at Congo Square
                i offer ceremonial tobacco to the grounds
            in exchange for dirt
        now on my altar
    overcome with prayers
for their return—

i had to lose everything to learn that nothing is ever lost

the moment i realized
        that i'd been heartbroken my whole life
            but so has everyone i've ever met
                was the moment everything changed

the way fear always leads you back to itself
        if you ride it long enough
            it grows thick with night

it's always raining when i leave New Orleans
i let it kiss my face & promise return
knowing no one else can bring my music
land back must feel like falling in love

✥

    land back radiating from my limbs
        quiet prophecy burning in my thighs
    land back in my sex
        feel it gathering lightning
            for the spirits to ride
                back into the ground
    land back like i can feel my marriage
        coming in slow motion
            lilac & jasmine dreaming into
                the unconquistador'd air
    land back a chant
        that becomes a vow
            that has no choice but to happen
    land back like falling in love
    land back a heartbeat into the kingdom
    land back humming heaven into the whispered day
    land back like falling in love
        earth & skin under-
            wind aching for it
                the unconquistador'd air is ours

[To Coda ✥ *lighter on the return]*

for my brother prelude & epilogue

Can you hear them?
Hear whom?
Can you hear the men in my chest?
They are sawing off a piece of my heart for Carrick.

A conversation between my mom & me in a letter that was
buried with my brother.

for my brother

the way you flew from that roof

    &

        split your skull on the street

            like falling in love

button poetry

Notes

Poetry is a political act because it involves telling the truth.

June Jordan

monarchs are the communication medium for when i die

for my grandmother Mere

Mère as in mother in French, but in Creole tradition some people call their grandmothers Mere—usually written without the accent in Creole. She was in many ways a second mother to me; I stayed with her in both New Orleans & the Mississippi Gulf Coast for parts of my childhood & adolescence. It was during a stay with her almost a decade ago that I started putting together this collection. A writer & illustrator of children's & young adult books who taught children's literature at Tulane, she was a phenomenal storyteller & I remember her stories about our ancestry & Louisiana history well. Many of them are woven throughout this book.

like Creole royalty holding our ground as it recedes beneath us

This is partially a reference to my second-great-grandfather Leonidas Pool who was King of Carnival in 1925, but what most needs clarifying is the meaning of *Creole*.

Creole is a very important & complicated word in Louisiana with a living history, so I want to illuminate both its earliest & most common use along with my own relationship to it. I initially intended this to be a brief explanation of the word, but quickly realized that honoring its complexity & significance meant a much deeper dive. Its use can vary in other parts of the world, but I'm concerning myself with its meaning in Louisiana.

According to Dr. Virginia Domínguez, professor of anthropology at University of Illinois at Urbana-Champaign & author of "Social Classification in Creole Louisiana," *"Jean-Bernard Bossu's* Travels in the Interior of North

America 1751-1762 *(1962)* marks the earliest published reference to Creoles in Louisiana proper" [emphasis added]. In discussing the types of people living in New Orleans & how locals referred to them, on July 1st, 1751, he wrote: "Those born of French fathers and French, or European, mothers are called Creoles. They are generally brave, tall, well-built and have a natural inclination towards the arts and sciences."

Creole derives from the Spanish *criollo*, from the verb *criar*, meaning to raise or bring up in this context. Dr. Domínguez notes that the Spanish "used it to refer to persons born of European parents in the islands as well as to locally born blacks." It's sometimes also traced back to the Portuguese *crioulo*, but in Louisiana, it most likely came from the much larger & more influential Spanish presence. The word was then Gallicized to *Créole* & soon after became *Creole* without the accent. According to the article "Creole History in New Orleans" on neworleans.com, "The term originally referred to the New World-born offspring of Old World-born parents" or ancestors—primarily referring to those of French & Spanish lineage. Dr. Domínguez says of its early use: "During the eighteenth century, Creole basically signified native born, as it did in other European colonies. ... The Creoles were defined ... by their local birth & European ancestry," which was sometimes mixed with African or indigenous ancestry as well. In a review of "Social Classification in Creole Louisiana," Dr. Paul Lachance, former professor of history at the University of Ottawa, writes, "Former free persons of color used the term Creole to mean either individuals of racially mixed ancestry, or all Louisianians with some French or Spanish ancestry, whatever their color." As Dr. Domínguez makes clear, "*Creole is defined by ancestry*" [emphasis added].

When referring to Creole as an ethnic identity, I define it as the descendants of the French, Spanish, Native Americans, & West Africans born in Louisiana as the culture & identity were forming in the 18th- & 19th-centuries. This definition is the most common in my experience as well as the one that I've most encountered in academic & historical texts. Based in part on the work of Dr. Domínguez & Dr. James Dorman, former professor of history at the University of Louisiana at Lafayette, Wikipedia has a definition of *Louisiana Creole* that mirrors mine & adds a historical marker for its use, "In Louisiana, the term Creole has been used since 1792 to represent descendants of African or mixed heritage as well as the children of French & Spanish descent with no racial mixing."

Defining it this way not only most accurately represents its longest historical use in Louisiana but honors the cultures & lineages that contributed to its creation without hierarchy. It also rescues it from later efforts to claim it as a term applied to those of exclusively French or Spanish ancestry from the region.

The term began to pick up significance & use in the 1790s with the arrival of refugees from Saint-Domingue where it was used to define those who were "locally born and had at least partial European ancestry," according to Dr. Domínguez. The Louisiana Purchase in 1803 catalyzed a slow shift in both demographics & racial identities—& brought with it new social & even legal implications for ethnicity & race. Dr. Domínguez writes, *"The Americanization of Louisiana strengthened the Creole identity. ... The Creoles banded together to oppose the American sector"* [emphasis added]. While most of the 19th- century saw the term applied regardless of color, by the 20th century, the local French were codifying it in their literature as exclusively for those of French (or sometimes Spanish) ancestry in the region who were "white." Despite the earlier 1869 edition of *Larousse* (Vol. V: 490-491), which is a comprehensive encyclopedia & French dictionary referenced to this day, stating that *Creole* was a term that applied to both "whites" & people of color, *Larousse du Vingtième du Siècle* (Vol. II), published in 1929, "restricted the term to the presumably white population." As Dr. Domínguez says, after centuries of colonialism enacted upon the population, "Race had achieved primacy over local birth as a criterion for classification."

Why would "white" Creoles attempt to restrict the definition of *Creole* & distance themselves from Creoles of color after so much shared history & culture? Dr. Domínguez attributes it to "a basic structural shift in the definition and hierarchical arrangement of social categories." The Anglo-Americans moving to New Orleans were, as she explains, *"suspicious of the Creoles' lack of stress on purity of white ancestry"* [emphasis added]. As some "white" Creoles sought to align themselves with the ruling class elite & thus the Anglo-American ideas of race starting to permeate New Orleans society, the Creole identity would undergo the same colonial assault that saw many other ethnicities subsumed by whiteness. However, unlike those other ethnicities, despite becoming more fractured, the Creole identity would not fully succumb to those forces.

Dr. Domínguez notes, as many have, that "Louisiana ... had always had a large population of free people of color." Creole people of color continued to identify as Creole despite attempts to exclude them from the identity. Thus, in later generations, some "white" Creoles would abandon the identity seeking further alliance with Anglo-Americans whom they had historically sought to distance themselves from. So, somewhat ironically, in part because of earlier attempts to codify it as a subset of the white identity, Dr. Domínguez points out that "a large number of New Orleanians today believe Creole signifies a light-skinned black of French and Spanish ancestry." Neither of these exclusive definitions accurately reflect its historical, cultural, or lived reality & both exclude those of primarily indigenous ancestry thus downplaying the essential contributions of Native Americans in Louisiana to Creole culture & history. In decolonizing it from these misappropriations, Creole is fully restored as an ethnicity that has the potential to undermine the myopic & often ahistorical identities that systems of oppression rely upon. As the beliefs of Dr. Noel Ignatiev, author of *How the Irish Became White*, are summarized in *The New Yorker*, "whiteness [is] a fiction & true stories [can] dispel it."

The relatives whose homes I lived in during my childhood—my grandmother Mere's & my great-grandmother Mimi's—referred to themselves as Creole. It's the only ethnic identity that I've ever claimed & the only one I've ever fully resonated with experientially, culturally, & ancestrally. For as long as I can remember, I identified with it on official forms like the census & standardized tests; I've long wanted to clarify & decolonize its meaning from its misconceptions.

Creole can also refer to the language, cuisine, music, architecture, & other cultural expressions created or adapted by Creoles—especially the language & food. The first dish I ever cooked for myself when I was around six or seven was pain perdu, or Creole French toast, following a recipe in my grandmother's book *Delicious Dishes: Creole Cooking for Children* (first published in 1983). Creole & Cajun are sometimes used interchangeably (even by locals), but they're distinct identities historically, culturally, & ethnically. Cajuns are specifically from Acadia, now Nova Scotia, New Brunswick, & Prince Edwards Island. After they refused to sign an unconditional oath of allegiance to Britain, the British began expelling them in 1755 in a campaign that lasted through 1764 with many Acadians eventually making their way to Louisiana. Thus, the Acadian refugees began arriving in Louisiana after the French & Spanish—& after the word *Creole* was already in use.

In *The Forgotten People: Cane River's Creole of Color,* Gary B. Mills, who was himself the descendant of Cane River Creoles & a professor of history at the University of Alabama, makes it clear that the Creole identity doesn't just apply to peoples of exclusively French & Spanish descent, but also includes those who have African ancestry "mixed" with either French or Spanish heritage: "It should be noted that considerable disagreement exists regarding the exact definition of the term Creole and the elements of Louisiana society to which this term should be applied. In this study, the term is used to signify any person born in the colony of French and Spanish descent (with the sole exclusion of the Acadian exiles—popularly called Cajuns—who settled in south Louisiana and maintained a separate ethnic identity). Creoles will not be limited herein to Louisianians of pure-white descent, to the wealthy aristocracy of the state, or to the residents of the New Orleans-Baton Rouge area exclusively, as has often been the restrictive usage." I love that Mills is careful to protect the Creole identity from any attempts to view it as exclusively "white." As Mills says, "*They claim a variety of racial origins: French, Spanish, Indian, and African. Their blend of cultures has been so assiduously cultivated and perpetuated that they have long been considered a distinct ethnic group within Louisiana's culture.*"

This blend of cultures is perfectly encapsulated in my first, clear memory: joining a second line dancing behind a marching band at a Mardi Gras parade near my grandparents' house. I saw the intricately adorned floats & elaborate headdresses of Mardi Gras Indians; throws of beads & doubloons sparkled & cascaded down from the sky landing all around me. All the cultures present in Louisiana's birth poured into a single moment.

self-portrait waiting for a body (nine & a half Royal)

kat er

Louisiana Creole (Kréyòl Lwizyàn) for four o'clock.

warriors from the Caddo nation heeded / my seventh-great-grandfather's beads once more ... they tattooed thick snakes round / his legs & named him / Kadolahoapi: / Chief Big Leg

Kadolahoapi means Chief Big Leg or Big Leg in Caddo & was the name the Natchitoches gave to my seventh-great-grandfather. *Kado, kahdu, kahdii, cado,* or *caddo*—depending on the phonetic transliteration—all mean chief or chiefs in Caddo. The Natchitoches speak their own dialect of Caddo also called Natchitoches.

Ethnohistorian Dr. David La Vere described this exchange about Chief Big Leg—recorded by François Grappe, the highest-ranking officer of the Natchitoches detachment—between the Spanish Captain / wannabe conquistador Gil Ybarbo & the Kichai, another Caddo tribe. After Gil claimed that the land west of the Red River belonged to him, a Kichai warrior threw dirt at him saying "that since the land was [his], [he] could take it with [him]." Ybarbo responded that he was "the great chief," to which the Kichai chief responded:

"[That] the real chief for [them] was the chief with the big leg. It was he who had first opened the trails in all their nations and who had made the peace and he who had provided all manner of help to [them]; [that] he had died; but [that] he had left one of his descendants, and [that] *it was him whom [they] regarded as [their] chief and [that] [they] would look the same way upon all his descendants, as long as there would be some*" [emphasis added].

Caddo historian & former Cultural Liaison for the Caddo Tribe of Oklahoma Cecil Elkins Carter refers to him as the "chief they called Big Leg" in the chapter "True Chiefs" in *Caddo Indians: Where We Come From*. Carter also describes Big Leg's relocation of the Natchitoches tribe from their ancestral lands after they flooded & became uninhabitable for several years. She also describes the Natchitoches, French, & two other Caddo tribes, the Cadohadacho & Hasinai, fighting the Spanish alongside one another under Big Leg's leadership—as well as the French-Natchitoches marriages, families, & new bloodlines that emerged during this time. "In time, the blood of some of these neighbors would blend to produce respected new families of French-Natchitoches parentage. The Natchitoches, Cadohadacho, and Hasinai tribes knew St. Denis as a man who could be trusted. He kept his promises."

In *The Louisiana Journey*, historian Dr. Terry L. Jones describes Big Leg's tattoos, "Several tribes honored St. Denis by tattooing his legs, which were thick and muscular. Colorful snake and serpent tattoos wound around them."

In exploring these historical realities & relating them to the present moment, there is a clear distinction between ancestral ties to indigenous peoples—even if they are thoroughly documented & substantiated—& claiming an indigenous identity or membership in an indigenous group.

i still hear the harmonies of Angola's chain gangs

Angola Prison Farm is the largest maximum-security prison in the US with over 6,300 prisoners. It is located on an 18,000-acre property that was previously the Angola Plantations. In 2012, *The Times-Picayune* called Louisiana "the world's prison capital—locking up more of its residents per capita than any other state in the union." It also noted, "A majority of Louisiana's inmates are housed in for-profit facilities, which must be supplied with a constant influx of human beings, or a $182 million industry will go bankrupt."

New Orleans at four

my father broke a glass milk jug fresh over the skull / of an armed robber / in our driveway / on a trip back from Langenstein's, / knocked him out cold / stomped his head into the concrete / took his gun & flight

After I wrote this poem, I heard a different version of this story where my father *threw* the glass milk jug at the armed robber in our driveway, then took off.

Mere wrote their stories in chalk crosses

She wrote a book called *The Chalk Cross*, in which a young girl in present-day New Orleans time travels to meet Marie Laveau & learns to reconcile Catholicism with her discovery of Voodoo.

on the steps of my other childhood home Pop called the sonofabitch / with the chopper in his belly a sonofabitch / threw cash in his face & walked away for he still / held the real heat

The other childhood home was my paternal grandparents' house, which was the only house where I stayed consistently throughout my whole childhood/adolescence (my parents lived in the upstairs of my great-grandmother's house in New Orleans before moving several times). I added the part about my grandfather Pop throwing his cash in the robber's face, but he did call him a "sonofabitch" (reported as calmly saying, "here you go, you sonofabitch," which definitely tracks), hand him some cash, & walk away.

lucid second line

Pop lifted me up by the nape of my neck for walking in front of a lady / painted & open at Zulu

This was three childhood memories I combined into one: my grandfather Pop lifting me up by the nape of my neck for walking in front of a woman when I was leaving an elevator, going to Mardi Gras parades with him when I was little, & going to the Zulu parade when I was a kid with neighborhood friends.

sha

Creole for the French *cher* meaning dear.

Rose's chicory café au lait

Rose Nicaud bought her freedom by establishing the first coffee stand in New Orleans in the early 19th century when New Orleans was the largest coffee port in the country.

Isaac Newton Marks / my third great / King of Carnival … leading the unification movement: / tinder merging with wind / waiting for a spark to carry

I'm conflating two ancestors here: 1) my second-great-grandfather Leonidas Pool, who was King of Rex, which is also known as King of Carnival as Rex is Mardi Gras's apex parade, in 1925; & 2) my third-great-grandfather

Isaac Newton Marks, who led the Unification Movement for racial equality & justice in post-Civil War New Orleans. More on him & the movement below:

Dr. Justin Nystrom, associate professor of history at Loyola University in New Orleans, describes my third-great-grandfather's & the Unification Movement's call for racial equality & justice in post-Civil War New Orleans, "The Unifiers went much further, however, advocating integration for public schools as well as private restaurants, taverns, and hotels ... and implored financial institutions and insurance companies to provide services without regard to race. Their manifesto bore a remarkable resemblance to the Civil Rights Act of 1964. ... Isaac Newton Marks played a strong leadership role." The Unification Movement was devised & brought to life by The Committee of One Hundred, which was composed of fifty Blacks & fifty "whites" & helmed by democratically elected leadership. Isaac Newton Marks was a founding member & the chair. He was born & raised Jewish but converted to Christianity. He's described in the 1873 book *Jewell's Crescent City, Illustrated* as a "gentleman of Hebrew descent."

poque

The original name for poker, which came to America through New Orleans.

Chief Bacate Batiste

The founder of the Creole Wild West tribe, which many consider the first Mardi Gras Indian tribe.

but to pretend to care about a decaying baby's bones from another century

"But race is the child of racism, not the father. And the process of naming the people had never been a matter of genealogy and physiognomy so much as one of hierarchy. Difference in hair and hue is old. But the belief in the preeminence of hue and hair, the notion that these factors can correctly organize a society and that they signify deeper attributes, which are indelible—this is the new idea at the heart of these new people who have been brought up hopelessly, tragically, deceitfully, to believe they are white."

Ta-Nehisi Coates, *Between the World and Me*

L'Ouverture sparked the sale of Louisiana / & launched steamboats carrying our name to Natchez

New Orleans was the first steamboat to operate in Western waters.

everything royal for a moment

walked pale creatures who thought they were real & white at once

"These new people are, like us, a modern invention. But unlike us, their name has no meaning divorced from the machinery of criminal power. The new people were something else before they became white—Catholic, Corsican, Welsh, Mennonite, Jewish—and if all our beliefs are to have national fulfillment, then they will have to be something else again."

Ta-Nehisi Coates, *Between the World and Me*

Camille 1969 & still

but Bob's boat sat in the boat shed waiting to sail round the world

He called his boat the *Mer Gris*.

watch out for falling bullets

kann lanmoutombé la encore

This is my translation into Louisiana Creole of *when the lovefall comes again*, which is itself my own molding of language to convey an idea, experience, & music. I took the *comes* out in the translation to make it more colloquial & because I prefer it sonically. I'm not fluent in Louisiana Creole; I know a handful of words & phrases. It's not spoken in New Orleans proper anymore—just in a few pockets in the Louisiana countryside & even there mostly among the older generations. I first heard Louisiana Creole as a young child in my grandmother's house from Mable, who isn't technically family, but is still fully family if you understand. I spoke to Mable a couple of times about my translation & she said it sounded correct to her in so much as the phrase itself is inventive & therefore harder to translate. Love can be said in a few different ways in Louisiana Creole. Some of the spellings aren't fully standardized, especially around the use of accents. It's similar to Haitian Creole, but not identical. I pray it thrives again in Louisiana, carried forward by future generations.

but if fire

i was slipping a cross

The "two," or dominant-hand cross, in a classic one-two boxing combination.

middle school & other initiations

Love & healing & empowerment to all the survivors.

i got kicked out of public schools in seventh grade

After my fifth out-of-school suspension that year, they told me they'd let me finish the year, but that I couldn't come back for eighth grade. I would've had to go to Mark Twain, the public school for kids who'd been kicked out of their district school.

i'd already been pumping since late that winter anyway

I wasn't moving weight or anything in seventh grade—mainly nickels & dimes, occasionally eighths & quarters at that point.

my best friend hated me

We used to hang a lot in middle school, especially seventh grade, & had sleepovers at each other's places regularly. He was one of my best friends at the time in the sense of time spent together, but, in retrospect, he for sure wasn't one of my closest friends in terms of real friendship.

i heard his dad had connects in Colombia

I heard his dad had international connects. I added the specificity of Colombia for the poem.

when he was killed in the middle of a house party / for smacking one of his runners around / everyone saw it coming

Rest In Peace. I hope he finds solace. He was so stormy, dark, & troubled when I knew him.

at least eight arrests that i can remember

It was really seven plus the threat of an eighth. The only two that were for anything serious were the two mentioned here—the grand theft auto plus the threat of arrest for distribution. For the former, charges were dropped after they found out I was twelve & just a backseat passenger. For the latter, I was questioned & threatened with arrest, but never charged. I had six arrests as an adult all in my late teens. One was for an illegal knife for which I was sentenced to community service cleaning parks. The other five were all for minor things like jumping a subway turnstile while having a bench warrant for an unpaid ticket for jumping a subway turnstile—still had to spend the night in The Tombs or Brooklyn Central though. Four of those overnight stays were routine, but two blessed me with some wild stories—one on Halloween night.

but i was just moving ounces

By eighth grade, I was buying ounces & either flipping them or breaking them down & reselling them.

Freddy & i laughed ourselves through the smoke / the last time he sold me a qp / he handed me an extra bag for free / right before Samuel Sheinbein / & Needle / killed him with a sawed-off / & burned the body / Sheinbein fled to Israel & the US somehow lost / the extradition battle to a country whose existence it funds

R.I.P. Alfredo Enrique Tello, Jr. He was older & wasn't a close friend, but we used to burn together sometimes & I'd cop weight from him on occasion—unquestionably a powerful presence & I really felt it when he died; not someone you forget.

The ensuing extradition battle after his murder taught me so much about the relationship between the US & Israel.

but the Carlos who got shot in front of his grandmother's / building in the summer between seventh & eighth grade

R.I.P. Carlos. He was always so happy to see me. I think we shared an empathy in part because we both hated bullies. He was a year older than me, so I was between seventh & eighth grade & he was between eighth & ninth grade when he got shot.

middle school & other initiations redux rant

i wasn't even a teenager when that cop slammed / my high head on the hood of his car

I was actually thirteen when this happened, but I wanted to keep the pattern of "I wasn't even a teenager" going.

the ecstasy of betrayal & other etymologies

Baba told me to be careful with my slow-lightning tongue

Credit the phrase *slow lightning* to Eduardo C. Corral; *Slow Lightning* is the name of his certified classic.

poetry is a party line

Tomás Q. Morín at a Bread Loaf lecture in 2023

New York: the portal to paradise at the end of time

Pablo Jeria would later say of New York's 9/11:

"Desde ese día del ataque, la psiquis de los NYorquinos ha cambiado ya no son tanto el equivalente al porteño Argentino, mandados las porciones, se han convertido en seres con verdaderas cualidades humanas y más cordiales con los extraños."

Translated to English: "Since that day of the attack, the psyche of New Yorkers has changed. They are no longer the equivalent of the Argentine porteño, who has been given the orders, they have become beings with true human qualities and more cordial with strangers."

after Simon Verity's Portal of Paradise *sculptures at Saint John the Divine Cathedral*

I added this epigraph on July 28th, 2024, & on August 11th, 2024, master sculptor Simon Verity died, which definitely felt a touch eerie as I wrote the first version of this poem years ago. He started carving the *Portal of Paradise* at Saint John the Divine in 1988 & finished it in 1997. R.I.P. Simon Verity. Thank you for all of the stunning work.

Jay Black ran up on me: ayo Phil, you heard? this shit is crazy / yeah, man, i know! i can't believe this, bro / yeah, man! this new Jay-Z album is fire!

I know I'm being very particular here, but it wasn't Jay Black who ran up on me. Jay Black (not his gov't, but how he was often called) was my upstairs neighbor in Harlem, but I can't remember the name of the dude who ran up on me that day. The conversation is verbatim though. It always stuck with me.

hoping for liberty in the nation / that helped take his birth country's

Nixon: "Our hand doesn't show on this one, though."

Kissinger: "We didn't do it. I mean, we helped them."

a twelve-panel progression answering all the big questions of / what time has carved for us at its end

The panels I'm referring to are just beneath the figures carved into a series of pillars in the west portal. There are six on either side of the double doors. There is another panel at the same height on the pillar in the center between the two sides of the progression, but it seems to stand alone (literally & thematically). I wasn't able to confirm the artist's intentions, & he just passed (R.I.P. Simon Verity). There's another sixty-panel progression on the double doors, but I'm not referencing that one.

the penultimate panel stops the breath inside us

This is actually the ninth panel in the progression. but I prefer penultimate sonically.

Thai snake bite

every banded sea krait that glides

I'm not 100% sure what kind of venomous snake bit me, but based on snakes native to the area, the neurotoxic effects of the venom I experienced, the size of the snake, the puncture wounds from the fangs & how they healed, & the color, I feel fairly confident that it was a banded sea krait. Their venom is roughly ten times more lethal than a rattlesnake's. They spend most of their time near coral reefs, but do come on land to nest, drink fresh water, rest, & digest their food. They're very non-aggressive & bites are rare, but bites do happen every year. It was partially submerged in sand & I accidentally stepped on it. There's an old wives' tale that their mouths are too small to bite people, but there's no truth to that. They don't always inject venom when they bite, but envenomated bites are usually fatal. I feel extremely blessed to have survived. If you're ever bitten by a venomous snake (you'll be able to tell immediately as only venomous snakes have fangs), if you can safely, take a picture because most antivenom, at least at time of writing, is specific to the species with only a handful of exceptions.

it promises to free that slow / lightning on rotation / on your radio every day

Again, credit the way of Eduardo C. Corral & his stunning first collection *Slow Lightning*.

we publish come hell & high water

you're a journalist riding

Based on a post-Katrina bike ride taken by James O'Byrne, features editor of *The Times-Picayune*, & Doug MacCash, art critic for the *Picayune*

i'm not shooting another picture until i rescue someone

Times-Picayune photographer Ted Jackson as quoted by Jim Amoss

the August air makes us slower than a sack of nickels

A New Orleans Saints employee to me: "Yeah, these tourists slower than a sack of nickels."

& let the levees / fall apart despite your warnings

Three years before Hurricane Katrina hit New Orleans, *The Times-Picayune* ran a five-part series about what would happen if there was a major hurricane, highlighting the need to improve the levee system, among other things.

the city will be chocolate at the end of the day

Mayor Ray Nagin on the city's recovery

land back on Tchoupitoulas (no one else can bring my music)

Chief Big Leg, bless the medicine chalice / before i drink again

See my earlier notes on "self-portrait waiting for a body (nine & a half Royal)" for information on my ancestor Chief Big Leg.

Acknowledgements

I'm writing this a few hours before I send this book back to the press for publication. It's a surreal moment. I started putting this collection together nine years ago in August 2015 while staying with my grandmother Mere. I wrote the oldest poem from it in 2011—although the version that appears here is very different from the one I wrote then. I feel almost certain I'll forget a thank you to someone essential so please forgive me if that's you.

I had the incredible luxury/privilege of having piles of notes & feedback on many of the poems from various workshops to look over as I was editing. They have been invaluable to me. Thank you to my workshop leaders & fellows at Bread Loaf: Carl Phillips & Gabrielle Bates, francine j. harris, Reginald Dwayne Betts & Delapo Demuren, Daisy Fried & Nicole Sealey. I carry your insights into everything I write. Thank you to the Desire Field: Cat Wei, Isabella DeSendi, Lily Greenberg, Philipe AbiYouness, Tawanda Mulalu, Hua Xi, Meagan Washington. I went through your notes over & over while editing. Thank you to Matthew Gellman for the insightful feedback on "self-portrait as past lives." Cat, thank you for answering all my questions so thoughtfully & generously; I feel infinitely blessed to receive your brilliance, wisdom, & support. Bella, thank you for your incredibly thorough notes & the fiery love you bring to them. Diana Cao, thank you for your illuminating perspectives, unbridled enthusiasm, & on-point suggestions.

Thank you to everyone who wrote advance praise for this collection: Darrel Alejandro Holnes, Cat Wei, Isabella DeSendi, Tawanda Mulalu, Megan Fernandes. I love that my book is graced with the words of friends—appreciate y'all endlessly.

Thank you to Bread Loaf Writers' Conference for believing in me & supporting me. I've gotten more than I could ever fully describe from those experiences. Thank you to Noreen, Jason, Lauren, & Jennifer—incredible what you do every year. To many more.

Thank you to Mable for reviewing the Louisiana Creole in my poems. Can't wait to see you again. Miss your face; miss your laugh; miss your gumbo.

Thank you to the poetry angels, guides, & teachers who've helped me navigate the world of contemporary poetry, especially when I was just starting to enter it: Marina Weiss, Monica Wendel, Sampson Starkweather, Itiola Jones, J. Scott Brownlee, Bianca Stone, Emily Skillings, Simone Kearney, & others.

Thank you to my family & ancestors. I return to you for support & inspiration over & over & you never fail. I'm forever grateful & humbled. Thank you to my dad for constantly correcting my grammar & questioning my word choices while I was growing up. It drove me crazy, but it sharpened my sword. Thank you for your feedback on the manuscript. Thank you to my mom for telling me my poems made her cry & always believing in me. Thank you to both my parents for the endless support & encouragement. Feel ridiculously lucky to have y'all as parents.

Thank you to the editors of the following journals for publishing earlier versions of poems that appear in this collection: *Poetry International, Tinderbox Poetry Journal, Voicemail Poems, Origins Literary Journal, Reality Beach, Sonic Boom Journal,* & *Alien Mouth Journal.*

Thank you to Button Poetry & Tanesha Nicole Kozler for believing in me; & for all the love & energy you've poured into this project. I feel so blessed to work with you.

Thank you to Pete Longworth for the stunning cover image. Nobody else can do what you do. Grateful for your vision & skills.

Thank you, most especially, to my readers. All poetry is co-created.

About the Author

Phil SaintDenisSanchez is a Creole poet from New Orleans. His work has appeared in *Poetry International, Tinderbox Poetry Journal*, and elsewhere. His poem "monarchs are the communication medium for when i die" was a finalist for *Poetry International*'s C.P. Cavafy Prize and his chapbook "watch out for falling bullets" was a finalist for *The Atlas Review*'s and Button Poetry's chapbook contests, and a notable manuscript for *BOAAT*'s chapbook contest. A semifinalist for the 2020 Discovery Prize, he has received scholarships to attend Bread Loaf Writers' Conference and presented at AWP on creating collaborations between poetry and music. He studied music theory and composition at The City College of New York, records under the name SaintDenisSanchez, and currently lives in Brooklyn.

Book Recommendations from the Author

The Crown Ain't Worth Much by Hanif Abdurraqib

Lit with the fire of witnessing a predatory hunger and constantly underscoring the vicious yet fallacious nature of human hierarchy, *The Crown Ain't Worth Much* opens with the prelude "On Hunger" that stunningly closes, "... in a city / soaked by / a death which fed / no one's hunger / the fire rising to kiss the / black belly of a night sky / each star a set of / gleaming and eager teeth." The force of this image hangs over the rest of the work even as the speaker finds transcendence in music—a liberator, but also a time marker, a signifier, and the exalted as in "Ode to Kanye West in Two Parts, Ending in a Chain of Mothers rising from the River" and "Ode to Drake, Ending with Blood in a Field." Music is omnipresent in Hanif's writing, which wields its own music—haunting like the lyrics, tunes, and ancestors he brilliantly evokes.

Black Movie by Danez Smith

Powerfully written in a colloquial, intimate tone that wastes no time on pretense, *Black Movie* takes the medium and world of cinema and conveys it in poetic form. Smith draws heavily from the collective cultural mythos—adapting it to an urban setting in poems like "LION KING IN THE HOOD" and "SLEEPING BEAUTY IN THE HOOD," which ends "All the red in this cartoon is painted with blood: / the apples, the velvet robes, Jamal's cold mouth." Danez slowly asserts more and more control over the cinematic metaphor for life: casting, rewriting, and adding directorial notes until the final poem, "DINOSAURS IN THE HOOD," which I'm tempted to quote from, but can only be described as a masterpiece.

OTHER BOOKS BY BUTTON POETRY

If you enjoyed this book, please consider checking out some of our others, below. Readers like you allow us to keep broadcasting and publishing. Thank you!

Bianca Phipps, *crown noble*
Natasha T. Miller, *Butcher*
Kevin Kantor, *Please Come Off-Book*
Ollie Schminkey, *Dead Dad Jokes*
Reagan Myers, *Afterwards*
L.E. Bowman, *What I Learned From the Trees*
Patrick Roche, *A Socially Acceptable Breakdown*
Rachel Wiley, *Revenge Body*
Ebony Stewart, *BloodFresh*
Ebony Stewart, *Home.Girl.Hood.*
Kyle Tran Myhre, *Not A Lot of Reasons to Sing, but Enough*
Steven Willis, *A Peculiar People*
Topaz Winters, *So, Stranger*
Darius Simpson, *Never Catch Me*
Blythe Baird, *Sweet, Young, & Worried*
Siaara Freeman, *Urbanshee*
Robert Wood Lynn, *How to Maintain Eye Contact*
Junious 'Jay' Ward, *Composition*
Usman Hameedi, *Staying Right Here*
Sean Patrick Mulroy, *Hated for the Gods*
Sierra DeMulder, *Ephemera*
Taylor Mali, *Poetry By Chance*
Matt Coonan, *Toy Gun*
Matt Mason, *Rock Stars*
Miya Coleman, *Cottonmouth*
Ty Chapman, *Tartarus*
Lara Coley, *ex traction*
DeShara Suggs-Joe, *If My Flowers Bloom*
Ollie Schminkey, *Where I Dry the Flowers*
Edythe Rodriguez, *We, the Spirits*
Topaz Winters, *Portrait of My Body as a Crime I'm Still Committing*
Zach Goldberg, *I'd Rather Be Destroyed*
Eric Sirota, *The Rent Eats First*
Neil Hilborn, *About Time*
Josh Tvrdy, *Smut Psalm*

Available at buttonpoetry.com/shop and more!

BUTTON POETRY BEST SELLERS

Neil Hilborn, *Our Numbered Days*
Hanif Abdurraqib, *The Crown Ain't Worth Much*
Olivia Gatwood, *New American Best Friend*
Sabrina Benaim, *Depression & Other Magic Tricks*
Melissa Lozada-Oliva, *peluda*
Rudy Francisco, *Helium*
Rachel Wiley, *Nothing Is Okay*
Neil Hilborn, *The Future*
Phil Kaye, *Date & Time*
Andrea Gibson, *Lord of the Butterflies*
Blythe Baird, *If My Body Could Speak*
Rudy Francisco, *I'll Fly Away*
Andrea Gibson, *You Better Be Lightning*
Rudy Francisco, *Excuse Me As I Kiss The Sky*

Available at buttonpoetry.com/shop and more!

FORTHCOMING BOOKS BY BUTTON POETRY

Ebony Stewart, *WASH*
L. E. Bowman, *Shapeshifter*
Najya Williams, *on a date with disappointment*
Daniel Elias Galicia, *Still Desert*
Hailey M. Tran, *an everyday occurrence*
Chelsea Guevara, *Cipota*
Meg Ford, *Wild/Hurt*
Jared Singer, *Forgotten Necessities*

Available at buttonpoetry.com/shop and more!